The Story of

GEORGE GERSHWIN

Books by David Ewen

The Story of
GEORGE
GERSHWIN

by

DAVID EWEN

Illustrated by GRAHAM BERNBACH

HOLT, RINEHART AND WINSTON

New York · Chicago · San Francisco

Published, August, 1943
Twentieth Printing, November, 1972

ISBN: 0–03–042170–5
PRINTED IN THE
UNITED STATES OF AMERICA

CONTENTS

ACKNOWLEDGMENTS

For permission to reprint material first published elsewhere, the author would like to express his gratitude to the following:

Merle Armitage for quotations from essays by DuBose Heyward, Rouben Mamoulian, and J. Rosamond Johnson which appeared originally in *George Gershwin*, edited by Mr. Armitage for Longmans, Green & Co.

Coward-McCann for a brief quotation by George Gershwin which appeared in *Revolt in the Arts*, edited by Oliver M. Saylor.

Alfred A. Knopf for a stanza from *Of Thee I Sing*, by George S. Kaufman, Morris Ryskind, and Ira Gershwin.

New York Times for a brief quotation by George Gershwin which appeared in the Sunday Drama Section.

Simon & Schuster for two quotations extracted from *George Gershwin* by Isaac Goldberg.

Stanford University Press for a brief quotation by George Gershwin appearing in *American Composers on American Music*, edited by Henry Cowell.

Paul Whiteman for a quotation appearing in his autobiography, *Jazz*, published by J. H. Sears & Co.

The author wishes also to acknowledge gratefully the advice and editorial assistance of Mrs. Elizabeth C. Moore.

The Story of

GEORGE GERSHWIN

CHAPTER I

"*I'll Build a Stairway to Paradise . . .*"

· 1 ·

THE noises of the street were punctuated by three sharp whistles. George walked over to the window. His friends were waving for him to join them.

"Look, fellows," he called to them. "I'm not coming down just yet. Gotta do something for my mother. I'll meet you round the corner, later."

His mother came in from the kitchen, looked at him solicitously, then touched his brow with the tips of her fingers. "What's the matter, George? Aren't you feeling well today?"

"I'm all right, Ma. Honest. I just don't feel like going down with the boys right now."

He looked pensively out of the window. Unconsciously he absorbed the sights and sounds of the street. Grand Street was one of the principal thoroughfares in New York's lower East Side. It was alive and vibrant with activity. In the distance could be heard the thunder of an approaching train on the elevated structure; then the screech of the wheels upon the tracks as the train came to a halt at Grand Street Station; finally, the rumbling of the departing train. Downstairs, horse-drawn wagons clattered on the cobblestones. From time to time, a streetcar passed by, picking up and disgorging passengers. The sound of children's voices further added to the clatter: "One, two, three, O'Leary," a girl's high-pitched voice recited as she skillfully jumped rope. "The last to get to the corner is a sissy," exclaimed one of a group of boys roller-skating on the sidewalk. "Throw to first. Throw to first. He's out!" came the shriek from one of the boys playing ball in the gutter, as he instinctively avoided the passing traffic.

"It just isn't like you, George, not to join your friends," continued his mother. "Are you all right?"

George turned his eyes from the street scene to his mother. "Ma, when will the piano get here?"

"So that's it!" His mother laughed softly. It was a warm, pleasant laugh and expressed her relief. "You're thinking that the piano is some great big toy, aren't you? Well, you can shake that out of your thoughts. You'll get tired of the piano sooner than you think. I'll bet by this time next week you won't even want to look at it!"

George did not seem to hear. "But when *is* it coming?"

"How should I know when it's coming? Am I a prophet or something? The man said it would get here some time after three o'clock today. Here it's already four, and it isn't here yet. But what am I wasting time for? I've got to finish my cooking before Papa gets home for supper."

Some minutes later a horse-drawn truck stopped in front of the house. George bent over the window-sill, saw that the truck belonged to the music store three blocks away, and emitted a victorious whoop.

"It's here, Ma—it's here!"

Carefully bundled in quilts and blankets like an old man protecting himself from a chill, the upright piano was hoisted on pulleys and gently pulled through the open window. The imperial position in the living-room, directly opposite the windows, had been cleared for it. It now stood there, its new wood shining.

George approached the piano, lifted the lid, and let his fingers brush across the gleaming keys. His mother was in the kitchen; he was alone in the room. He sat down on the stool and began playing. The left hand moved awkwardly in octaves: C-C . . . G-G . . . C-C . . . G-G. . . . From the right hand, the sprightly measures of a popular tune leaped from his fingers, "Put Your Arms Around Me, Honey, and Hold Me Tight."

His mother rushed in from the kitchen, a wooden mixing spoon in her hand.

"Where did you ever learn to play the piano, George? I didn't think you even knew a piano from a washboard."

George explained diffidently: There had been a piano at the home of his friend. Often, while waiting for him, George would try his fingers on the keys, would experiment with the sounds, and would try to co-ordinate them into patterns of familiar melodies.

"If you *really* want lessons later on, George," his mother said, profoundly impressed by the exhibition, "I guess we'll be able to manage. Maybe the teacher we get for Ira will also give you lessons at the same time for a few cents more." Then, as an afterthought, she added: "But I don't think you'll want to have much to do with the piano before long. It's a novelty now and you like to play with it. But later on you'll be sick to death of it."

George was not listening. His fingers were experimenting on the keyboard. He was busy playing, trying out one gay tune, discarding it, then working on another. Finally, an appealing little melody assumed shape and outline.

"What's that you're playing, George?"

"That?" answered George dreamily. "That isn't anything much. It hasn't got a name. It hasn't even got an ending—yet. It's just something I wrote while trying out my friend's piano. I wanted to see if I remembered it."

· 2 ·

When George's father came home from business that evening and heard about George's exploits on the piano he burst into a good-natured laugh.

"I'm afraid, Rose, that a musical prodigy is one thing our George isn't." The thought of George as a musical prodigy brought on a second fit of laughter. "Maybe he's a prodigy something else—a roller-skater, maybe, or a punchball player. But a musician? . . . Paderewski doesn't have to be afraid of our George!"

"You do talk foolishness, Morris," his wife said petulantly. "How can you be so sure of yourself anyway? Besides, who said anything about a prodigy? I just said that George likes music, and if he likes music he ought to be taking lessons—*study* music."

"Give him lessons if you want to, but I can tell you now, that our George is no Paderewski."

Papa Gershwin was sure of himself, surer than he had ever been of anything. The millennium, he felt, was a brighter and nearer prospect than that George would ever become a musician.

For one thing, Papa Gershwin knew that, though the Gershwin family revealed many admirable traits, a talent for music was certainly not one of these. In Russia, the Gershwins had frequently proved their honesty, resourcefulness, business acumen. One of them (George's grandfather on his mother's side) had been a successful furrier. Another Gershwin had developed a new model gun which he had sold to the Czar for a handsome figure. No, the Gershwins had not been without their modest share of honor. Yet not even family pride (or a natural aptitude for exaggeration) would permit Papa Gershwin to distort sincerity to a point where he could say that his ancestors had shown a bent for things artistic.

As for Papa Gershwin himself, his musical gift consisted in making queer musical sounds by blowing into the teeth of a comb or by whistling through the open space of a clothespin. These antics—with which Papa used to burlesque opera arias—always inspired shouts of merriment whenever they were performed for visitors in the Gershwin living-room; but they hardly belonged in the category of good music. Papa Gershwin had no delusions on that score, at least. Gershwin blood was *not* musical blood. . . .

Besides, his boy George had already given every visible sign of being a true Gershwin. He was not an exceptionally bright boy. He disliked school lustily. His deportment in class was so lamentable that regularly, once every week, his older brother Ira was summoned to make hasty explanations to George's teacher and to promise reform. George evaded homework. He saw no point in reading books—not even the paper-covered thrillers which other boys (his brother Ira among them) devoured so hungrily. The world of art was as remote from his sphere of interests as China; possibly farther, for at least he had heard of China. Music for him consisted exclusively of the popular ballads of the day (though even in these he was not particularly interested), the snatches of melodies he heard from street hurdy-gurdies and carrousels, and a few sedate tunes like "Annie Laurie" and "Loch Lomond" which he was taught in school. Good music he avoided like the plague (though on the few isolated occasions when he was thrust into contact with it he had reacted favorably). George used to say that those who cultivated music were either girls or "Maggies." Only a "sissy," he felt, would abandon boyhood sports for piano-practice. *He* was made of sterner stuff; made for the games of the streets and the companionship of other virile boys. Up to his tenth year, therefore, he was sublimely innocent of any important musical influences or contacts.

This, then, as Papa Gershwin thought he knew only too well, was no musician in the making!

· 3 ·

As children, most of the great composers moved in the picturesque settings of European cities. Their early years were rich with tales of wonderful musical achievements. They seemed to live in a world of their own making, a world removed from the one in which other children grew and developed—a world built by imagination, fantasy, dreams.

But the story of George Gershwin's boyhood is far different. Not a picturesque Old World town was his background, but the noisy, dirty, crowded streets of a great American city. The sky, cramped by the roofs of tall buildings and generally clouded by soot and smoke, was the only everyday glimpse he could get of Nature. For a sight of green, city children like George made expeditions to public parks where Nature was as much on exhibition as the animals in the cages of the zoo: "Keep Off the Grass" . . . "Do Not Pick the Flowers." . . . Not trees, flowers, hills, brooks, woods, and singing birds made up George's childhood world—as it made up the childhood world of practically every other great composer—but gutters littered with refuse and swarming with pushcarts and passing traffic.

George's early experiences were not different from those of any other normal boy. No tales of fabulous musical exploits can be told of his earliest years: he was no prodigy, and excited no admiration or awe among those who knew him. His daily activity was that of almost every other growing American child. George was the son of the city. He was a part of feverish New York, breathing its air, absorbing its noises, responding to its excitement. His pulse and heartbeat were quickened by the tempo of city life. Almost every other American who has lived in a metropolis will find a reflection of his own early biography in George's boyhood.

(If you will listen to the *Rhapsody in Blue* and compare it with the music of Haydn, Mozart, Beethoven, Schubert, or Mendelssohn, you will at once recognize how different was the world in which George grew up from those of other composers. Their music speaks of the past, a past called up by story books and legends and beautiful paintings. George's music speaks of ourselves, our times, our experiences. It is as timely as the radio and the transatlantic Clippers.)

George had every opportunity to learn New York intimately—every corner of it—as a boy. Because

Papa Gershwin liked walking to work, and because the locale of his business changed frequently, the family often moved from one part of the city to the other. George was born on September 26, 1898, in Brooklyn, a few minutes from where the Williamsburg Bridge was then being built, the great bridge that in a few years was to span the East River and link the Williamsburg section with Manhattan. When he was still an infant, his family crossed the bridge and settled in the lower East Side of New York, the slums of the city, which particularly then was the melting pot of races and nationalities: immigrants coming from every part of the Old World streamed towards it—like iron filings to a magnet—and settled there permanently. After this, George lived in many different parts of the city: Harlem, again the East Side, again Brooklyn, again the East Side. It has been estimated that up to the time of his eighteenth birthday, he had lived in twenty-eight different apartments, twenty-five of them in New York, the other three in Brooklyn.

But change of residence did not cause any great upheaval in his way of living. Whether he lived uptown or downtown (the best years of his boyhood were spent in the lower East Side), his home was invariably in a large tenement house. The confusion of the city streets would fill the rooms with its chaotic noises; the dust of the streets would settle on the furniture. Frequently, the rumble of nearby elevated train or a horse-drawn streetcar would make the dishes rattle in their closet. The rooms were usually dark, and overcrowded with furniture. The windows would look out upon other ugly tenement buildings. It was not an aesthetic background, but George throve none the less. He seemed oblivious of the ugliness surrounding him. He was concerned only with the manifold pleasures which the city streets had to offer an athletic boy.

He was well built and muscular; there was nothing of the effete and sensitive prodigy about him. His body and spirit were hardened by life spent on city streets. He enjoyed roller-skating and was, as a matter of fact, one of the most skillful skaters in the neighborhood. He frequently played punchball, "cat," and hockey. Whatever he indulged in, he was of more than average competence. More frequently than not, he was the leader of the street's activities. In quieter moments, particularly after sundown, he would stand on the street corner discussing with his friends the prowess of the baseball idols of the day, particularly those on his favorite team, the New York Giants.

Though a few of his street associates were made of tougher fiber than he (some of them graduated from the city streets to reform schools and prisons), they generally respected him. George could give and take with the best of them. He indulged fearlessly in street fights and could take punishment without whimpering, but was usually capable of administering a severer dose than he got.

Besides the athletic pleasures of the streets, there were the delights of the nickel arcades where George could listen to popular songs of the day by plugging two rubber tubes into his ears and dropping a nickel into the slot. There were periodic afternoons spent at the neighborhood nickelodeon, the Unique Theatre on Grand Street, where pictures flickered and stumbled on a screen to the accompaniment of a booming piano. When Papa Gershwin was financially expansive, there might be an evening spent at a minstrel show, or in a music hall at Union Square. During the hot summers, the Gershwin family sometimes took an excursion to Coney Island, where the attractions— beyond surf bathing—were riding on the carrousel, and feasting on hot-dogs.

Fortunately for George—and for American music—the cruder experiences of the street were tempered and mellowed by influences at home. Both Papa and Mamma Gershwin had that deeply ingrained respect for culture which had always been a hereditary trait of their race. They created at home an atmosphere in which books and learning were revered. Ira had been designated for a college education and a professional career. George, too (his rebellion against the discipline of school notwithstanding), would have the advantages of learning.

Papa Gershwin was a simple man, with soft eyes, round face, and a lovable, gentle smile. He had a healthy respect for money. In his native St. Petersburg he had seen too much poverty at his elbow not to acquire a perhaps exaggerated esteem for the power of wealth. He had come to the land of opportunity because, like most immigrants, he had heard that with intelligence and industry one could acquire a fortune. Here in America, his life had been dedicated to the pursuit of material success. He was always on the alert for new opportunities. He exchanged one business venture for another, each time convinced that his new undertaking would at last spell prosperity. At various periods in his life he had been the owner of a cigar store, a bakery, a restaurant, a billiard parlor, a Turkish bath, a Russian bath. For a brief period he was even a "bookie" at the Brighton Beach racetrack. It seemed to his family that every six months he had a different or a greater business venture up his sleeve. Sometimes he made money, though never in sizable quantities; more often, he lost it. But always was he confident that his next undertaking would be the one to bring him straight into the awaiting arms of wealth.

He pursued money and success, yet he was not altogether a materialist. He had never had an education himself; but he was determined that his children would have one. The finer things of life eluded him;

but he would bring them to his sons and daughters. If George were miraculously to show a talent for music, Papa Gershwin—for all his outward cynicism—could be depended upon to spend the last coin in his pocket to pay for music lessons.

Mother Gershwin had married George's father when she was sixteen years old. They had met in St. Petersburg, but their marriage had not taken place until both of them had come to New York. Their first child, Ira, was born one year after their marriage. Next came George, two years younger than Ira. Then Arthur and Frances completed the family circle.

Mother Gershwin was a wise, gentle woman, with a heart that continually overflowed with affection. She was altogether incapable of an unkind thought. Though she never knew a formal education, she had a wisdom that comes not from study but rather from sharpness of perception and understanding and from instinctive good sense. She was hardworking and uncomplaining, as capable of maintaining a decently conducted household on little as on much. When there was money to spare she did not spoil her children with extravagances. When there was little or no money she saw to it—through the industry of her two strong hands, and her shrewd capacity to run a household—that her children were not denied any of the necessities of living.

She ruled her children with a gentle hand, guiding them, giving them all the benefits of her good sense and experience; but she could never be the disciplinarian. When George neglected his homework for play in the streets, she would understand and smile. If she objected to some of his companions, she might make her objections articulate, but she never forced the issue. She was a beautiful woman—not even housework and the raising of children were to rob her of her freshness and charm; and she was young. From early in his life, George adored her. "You know," George frequently said later in life, "my mother is the kind of woman they write mammy songs about. Only—I *mean* them."

· 4 ·

While George was at play in the New York streets, great changes were taking place in the world about him. The old century, which had died only a few years earlier, had transformed America into a world power, following the successful culmination of the Spanish war. The new century was to convert America into an industrial power without equal.

The railroad now stretched from one coast line to the other, making the entire country more compact and accessible. Towns arose where once had been barren spaces. Population increased in rapid spurts. Commerce spread. In every part of the country were growth and expansion felt. In the West, science had helped to bring greater richness of production to agriculture. In the South, new industries were recreating villages into throbbing factory cities. In the East, big business was encouraging the spirit of enterprise. The trust was growing fatter and fatter through the absorption of smaller businesses; the Sherman Anti-Trust Law, passed to prevent its fabulous expansion, was temporarily forgotten.

The hunger for wealth was sharpened everywhere, when fortunes came overnight to many as gold was discovered in Alaska and speculation intensified on the stock market, bringing fortunes overnight to many. So also with the hunger for success: initiative, "go-getterism," rugged individualism were the spirit of the new century, and, like Horatio Alger heroes, young men were convinced that with work and application anybody could conquer the world.

To George's home city, New York, as to most great American cities, the new age introduced far-reaching changes. The craze for speed began. In 1900, New York's first subway was opened. The automobile was gradually replacing the horse and the bicycle. The Wright brothers and Glenn Curtiss had proved that aviation was not the fantasy of idle dreamers. A new feverish tempo set in for everyday living, symbolized by the hurrying crowds in the city streets. Even entertainment began to move at a faster pace.

The minstrel show had been succeeded by the faster moving variety show and the musical comedy; and there were those who said that the recently invented "flickers" would soon displace the sluggish living theater. And in popular music, ragtime pushed the sentimental ballad of the 1890s into the discard.

The first skyscraper—the Flatiron Building at the intersection of Fifth Avenue, Broadway, and 23d Street in New York City—rose in 1902, the first indication that henceforth the modern city would grow upward rather than horizontally. Technology in the form of electricity, the telephone, and the phonograph was bringing to many an easier or a richer life.

The printed word was acquiring greater influence through the national circulation of best-selling novels (*The Crisis* sold 300,000 copies), magazines (*McClure's, Munsey's, The Saturday Evening Post*), and powerful newspapers. Through the printed word Americans everywhere were made conscious of the miraculous development of their country. They grew more interested in it, prouder of its achievements, less inclined to look across the Atlantic Ocean for models to copy. American novelists—Jack London, Edith Wharton, Frank Norris—were devoting themselves more and more to American scenes and experiences. Walter Damrosch had already composed an American opera to an authentically American libretto—*The Scarlet Letter.*

George was, of course, too young to know what was happening all around him. Yet, like every other American, his entire life was to be profoundly influenced by these contemporary changes. He was growing up together with twentieth-century America—the America whose most eloquent musical interpreter he was later to become.

· 5 ·

Years before the piano entered the Gershwin living-room, George had been made aware of good music. Because in the street the cultivation of music was looked upon as an effeminate pastime, he tried to outlaw it from his life. But the effort failed: try as he would, he could not help being fascinated whenever he came into contact with it, however briefly. Music cast a spell before which he was helpless.

One of his most vivid boyhood experiences was the accidental hearing of a piece of music. He was six years old at the time. "I stood outside a penny arcade listening to an automatic piano leaping through Rubinstein's *Melody in F*," he later recalled to his biographer Isaac Goldberg. "The peculiar jumps in the music held me rooted. To this very day I can't hear the tune without picturing myself outside the arcade on 125th Street, standing there barefoot and in overalls, drinking it all in avidly."

He had his first love affair when he was nine years old, the adored one being a shy little girl with smiling eyes and dimpled chin. George would not confess it to himself, but what had attracted him to her was her lovely voice, as delicate as the pipings of a flute. He would visit her and impatiently wait for her to sing for him. When she did, he lost all sense of reality. He thought he had fallen in love with the little girl, and, true to his age, he was heartily ashamed of himself. He *had* fallen in love; not with the girl, but with music.

His next vivid musical impression came to him at this same time—apparently in about 1908 or 1909. He was attending Public School No. 25 on the lower East Side, where one of his fellow-pupils was a violin prodigy named Maxie Rosenzweig (later to be well known on the concert stage as Max Rosen). Maxie gave a concert for the school in the auditorium. George, faithful to his assumption of contempt for music, would not attend. He preferred spending the time in the schoolyard with a game of ball. While playing, he clearly heard the sound of Maxie's violin through the open window. Maxie was playing the Dvořák *Humoresque*. His warm, tender tone thrilled George. As the melody took on shape and form for George he suddenly began to lose all interest in the ball game. Hardly aware of what was happening to him, he listened spellbound. He had never before heard anything so beautiful. "It was to me a flashing revelation!"

Still under the potent spell of the music, George was determined to meet its maker. He had forgotten that he considered anyone who had anything to do with music a "Maggie." He knew only that he had never wanted to meet anybody so much as this wonder-boy who could play such music on his violin.

George stood outside the school and waited for the young violinist—for Maxie was a year younger than George himself. He did not know what he would say to him when they met; but meet him he must—this George knew. As he waited the sky over-head darkened. A flash of lightning momentarily split the heavens, and rain descended with savage fury. But George did not move from his post. He refused to leave without talking to the young musician. He himself did not know why that inner force within him was keeping him there so stubbornly—his wet clothes clinging unpleasantly to his body, his teeth chattering with the chill—when good sense dictated that he should find refuge indoors.

A half-hour passed; then an hour. No sign of Maxie Rosenzweig. The rain had subsided into a slow but steady drizzle. Suddenly the sickening thought occurred to George that something had gone wrong with his plans, that Maxie must have left the building through some other exit. George rushed into the school building and made inquiries. Yes, they told him, Maxie had gone home quite a while ago, using the teachers' exit. Yes, they added, they could give him Maxie's address.

On making his way to Maxie's home, he learned that Maxie had already come and gone. The disappointment tightened the muscles of his face, and, in spite of his effort to control himself, his lips trembled. He stood there in front of the open door, awkward, drenched to the skin, embarrassed, not knowing what next to say or to do.

Maxie's mother, who had opened the door for him, inquired: "Are you a friend of Maxie's? I don't remember ever having seen you."

"No—I don't even know him. I wish I did." George hesitated a moment, then added: "You see, Mrs. Rosenzweig, I heard him play the violin today and I just *had* to tell him how much I admire him."

"Come back tonight after seven," Maxie's mother said kindly. "You can meet Maxie then. I'm sure he'll be proud and happy to know you."

From the first, the two boys took to each other. Maxie was flattered by George's undisguised admiration. Besides, he liked George's sincerity and warmth. On his part, George had never before met anyone quite like Maxie. Small, slight, sensitive, with shining intelligent eyes, and a flow of conversation that seemed inexhaustible, Maxie was far different from the boys he knew in the street. Maxie fascinated George with his enthusiasm—not over ball games or prizefights, but over music and musicians. And George listened, spellbound. They would walk arm in arm, up one street, down the next, concerned with no destination, oblivious to the street noises and to the rush of passing crowds. Maxie told George about Beethoven who, deaf, wrote the most wonderful music ever conceived by man; about Schubert, starving and unrecognized, writing one masterpiece after another as easily as man breathes; about Robert Schumann and his beautiful love for Clara which inspired him to achieve new heights in his creation. Then there were times when Maxie played for George, melodies like the "Ave Maria" of Schubert or "On Wings of Song" by Mendelssohn, melodies so beautiful that at moments George found it hard to breathe. A strange new world opened for him, and as he contemplated it he gaped with wonder and admiration. It was a world which made all others he had known seem drab by comparison.

A perceptible change now came over George. His friends realized it; his family only guessed it. The pleasures of the street no longer held for him their one-time fascination—the brawls, the roller-skating, the ball games, the companionship of rowdies, and the heated discussions about baseball players. He became more thoughtful and moody. When he could not be with Maxie he preferred sitting alone in the

Gershwin living-room bringing back to mind all that Maxie told him about music.

Then came the greatest pleasure of all. One of his friends was the proud possessor of a piano—an instrument that was then a luxury not found in many living-rooms of the East Side; it was to be several months before the Gershwins would have one of their own. Once, while visiting his friend, and while waiting for him to finish his supper, George sneaked up to the piano and pressed the keys. After a few hasty experiments, he tried to play. Success exhilarated him. He felt the inward glow of satisfaction warming his entire body. Before long he tried to make up a piece of music of his own.

From that time on, he was a frequent visitor at the home of his friend. Playing that piano made his heart throb with excitement; the street games were never like this! The mere anticipation of spending some time at the piano made the blood rush to his face. As he worked out one melody, then another, he felt the excitement of exploration. Each note was a step in the stairway that seemed to lead him to paradise.

No one knew that George had secretly acquired the elements of piano-playing. But the secret burned within him, demanding to be revealed. To whom? His friends of the street could hardly be expected to understand; they would only make fun of him. For a while, George thought of telling his family. He hesitated because he feared that they might treat this miracle flippantly. There remained only one person who would surely appreciate what had come over him. One afternoon, George confided in Maxie Rosenzweig.

"But that's wonderful, George!" Maxie cried excitedly. "You *must* play for me. You might have talent, great talent!"

So presently, at a neighbor's house, George played for Maxie: first some popular tune of the day, then a thing of his own. He played from his heart. The music swelled under his fingers. To George it was the most wonderful music in the world. When he had finished—

Maxie walked over to the piano and put his hand on George's shoulder. "I'm sorry, George," he said apologetically and with some difficulty. "I'm really awfully sorry. But I just can't lie to you. I know you want the truth. . . ."

"Yes, Maxie?"

"You just haven't any talent at all," Maxie told him. "*I* know. You'd better forget all about music. Take my word for it. You just haven't got it in you at all!"

· 6 ·

Maxie's verdict stabbed George with a pain whose sting was not soon forgotten. His pride had been hurt: he had made a fool of himself, and before one whom he admired more than anybody else! His first impulse was to take Maxie's advice and to abandon every thought of music permanently. For a while he actually refused to touch the piano at his friend's home. He returned to his playmates of the street and tried to recapture his old zest for their games. But he found that his thoughts roamed. In spite of himself, he was always humming tunes, thinking music, dreaming about the great composers. Then he arrived at his decision: talent or no talent, he now belonged to music. He returned to the piano and to thoughts of music-making. It brought him endless pleasure and satisfaction—wasn't that all that mattered, after all? George respected Maxie's opinion profoundly. If Maxie said he had no talent, George believed him implicitly. But he had found too much joy in making music to relinquish that joy now. He decided to cling to it desperately.

George had met the first crucial test of the true artist; and he triumphed. He had encountered discouragement and did not permit it to kill his enthusiasm for music permanently.

His decision was further strengthened when (miracle of miracles) a piano entered his home. George's aunt had some time earlier bought a piano for her children, and now his mother wanted one for *her* family. Actually, the Gershwin piano was acquired with Ira in mind; Mamma Gershwin had been lamenting Ira's lack of musical culture. But no sooner had it invaded the Gershwin household than George adopted it, and very soon he astonished his mother by sitting down before it—this twelve-year-old boy!—and playing some tunes. Presently he was to astonish her still further by begging for piano lessons.

From the neighborhood, a Miss Green was recruited for the purpose. She introduced George to official piano study by way of Beyer's *Exercises*, charging fifty cents a lesson. From that moment on, George and his piano were inseparable. His friends, calling to him from downstairs, no longer offered him the least temptation to join them in the streets. Even dull scales acquired romance in his eyes. Then, when his practice period was over, he could allow himself the wonderfully sensuous joy of letting his fingers wander aimlessly over the keyboard, producing strange, fascinating sounds of his own creation. The rhythms would leap, guided by some inner force which George could not explain. The melodies would have a poignant quality. George was speaking his heart through his newly discovered language.

But Miss Green's capacity as a teacher seemed restricted exclusively to Beyer. When George had gone through that volume, another teacher, with a wider scope, had to be found. Then still another. George was beginning to grow ever more critical of himself, his playing, his teachers.

Then the leader of a Hungarian band in the East Side—a Mr. Goldfarb—was engaged for what seemed to the Gershwins a fabulous fee, $1.50 a lesson. By now, the Gershwins were convinced of George's flair for music, and were ready to procure the best instruction to be had on the East Side. Mr. Goldfarb had a piano system all his own which he would describe at length to whoever would listen. He did not believe in scales. He did not believe in exercises. A pupil, he said, must learn music by playing music—not by subjecting himself to rhetorical nonsense. He fed George exclusively on a diet of potpourris from the Italian operas. Mr. Goldfarb was sentimental about Italian operas. He liked to play the arias with exaggerated retards, rubatos, and strange changes of tempo as the whim occurred to him, and he wanted his pupils to emulate him.

"I feel this music here," he would say, tapping his heart with the palm of his hand. "I must make *you* feel it that way, too."

Mr. Goldfarb and George did not have much respect for each other's gifts. To Mr. Goldfarb,

George appeared impulsive, headstrong, and recklessly frank. But what really piqued the bandleader was that this young upstart did not show the proper reverence and awe towards his teacher's musical position and erudition. George suspected that there was something radically wrong about Goldfarb's system. Instinctively he guessed that Goldfarb's eccentricities as a pianist were artistically lamentable. It was not long before the search began anew for a teacher. This search, when it ended, brought George the greatest single influence in his musical life: Charles Hambitzer.

The two were introduced by a friend of both who prevailed upon George to exhibit his talent to Hambitzer, already distinguished as a concert pianist and as a composer of operettas. George played the *William Tell* Overture in the manner recently taught him by Goldfarb. When George finished playing, Charles Hambitzer said firmly:

"Listen—you and I will now go out and hunt up the teacher who taught you to play that way. We'll shoot him—and without an apple on his head, either."

But Hambitzer, who was an astute and discerning musician, recognized that behind the exaggerated flourishes and overstressed climaxes of George's playing, there lurked something which impressed him profoundly. It was, perhaps, George's enthusiasm; or else his sincerity; or even his open-hearted love of music. These qualities shone in every phrase and bar, were reflected in every shading and nuance.

A few weeks later, when George had become his pupil, Hambitzer was to write to his sister: "I have a new pupil who will make his mark in music if anybody will. The boy is a genius, without a doubt; he's just crazy about music and can't wait until it is time to take his lesson. No watching the clock for this boy! He wants to go in for this modern stuff, jazz and what-not. But I'm not going to let him for a while. I'll see that he gets a firm foundation in the standard music first."

Charles Hambitzer not only taught George the piano: he encouraged him to go to concerts. And from this time on, George saturated himself with music in every concert hall in the city, wherever there was good music to be heard and whenever he had a few coins with which to buy a ticket. Hambitzer played for George the works of Chopin and Debussy, explained to him what there was in them that betrayed the hand of genius. He made George conscious for the first time of harmony and counterpoint, a fabulous new realm of sound for the boy. It was Hambitzer who was responsible for George's later studies in theory with Edward Kilenyi.

George frequently said, later in life, that he was "crazy" about Hambitzer. It was one of the tragedies of his life that, by the time he achieved his greatest triumphs as a composer, the man who had been the first to have faith in him and his gifts, who was the first to prophesy a great future for him, was no longer alive to see the fulfillment of his prophecy—for Charles Hambitzer had died of tuberculosis at the age of thirty-seven.

On one subject, and one subject alone, George and his teacher disagreed—and that was popular music. Hambitzer looked upon popular American music with the condescension, if not contempt, of the trained musician. He saw in it only naïveté, immaturity, vulgarity, ignorance.

"Don't you see, George," Hambitzer would argue with George almost pleadingly, "that the people who write these songs have no feeling whatever for musical beauty, no musical instinct, no imagination, no taste? Their songs bear the same relation to the music of Chopin and Schubert that jingles and limericks bear to the poetry of Keats and Shelley. It is hack stuff—and very poor hack stuff at that."

But George, usually so pliable under Hambitzer's influence, remained strangely firm in his own convictions. He was crazy about popular songs, and he was not ashamed of his passion. He now learned every new tune that came his way. He seemed to realize dimly that beyond the obvious simplicities of these songs there lay something strong and important, something that eluded even Hambitzer: a native musical expression that belonged to America alone. To this expression, George responded with all his instincts. The rhythmic freshness of ragtime—Irving Berlin's "Alexander's Ragtime Band" was a current hit—made his heartbeat quicken. He felt that a good musician (could he have been thinking of himself?) might use this American idiom and fashion a musical speech of importance and originality.

He loved the classics; Hambitzer's teaching had not been in vain. But American popular music—this, he began to feel, was *his* music. The world of the classic composers, beautiful though it was, was a different world from the one George knew: an old world, sedate, serene, well-mannered, inspiring him to quiet reveries. But this son of the city streets was coming to understand better and better that American popular songs expressed the things that formed *his* everyday experience, spoke *his* language. It was a sure instinct that led him to guess that, if there was any place for him in music at all, it lay in the field of popular music. Maxie Rosenzweig had been right: George was not meant to be serious composer or serious concert pianist. But what Maxie could not suspect was that George was born to write America's popular music.

Already George had composed a few songs of his own, and the popular song seemed the only natural medium. One of these songs, a tango, had actually reached public performance. The Finley Club of the

College of the City of New York, of which Ira was a member, gave a concert at Christodora House on the East Side, and George was on the program, playing a song of his own.

It was now that he decided to learn everything he could about the popular idiom. The only "conservatory" at which such an education could be acquired was—Tin-Pan Alley, the New York street where the songs of the nation were manufactured. He would enter Tin-Pan Alley as an apprentice hand and would learn everything he could about popular music. Once this idea took root in George's mind he grew impatient with school. The business courses he took at the High School of Commerce began to chafe him. Of what use were bookkeeping, typewriting, stenography to a boy with music in him, music that cried to be given life?

He confided his plans to his mother. From her, he felt, he could expect a sympathetic ear and understanding. So she listened to him, she smiled sadly. Because she did not speak at once, George knew that she was not with him.

"George," she said presently, "a boy without education is nothing at all. If you want to be a composer, I won't stand in your way. But first learn a profession so that you can earn a living like a decent human being. You can't make money out of music."

"But, Ma, can't you understand? If I'm to become a composer—a good composer, the kind of composer of popular songs that I feel I *can* be—I've got to learn everything I can about it! The education I want can't be found in ledgers. I want to learn everything I can about popular songs. That takes time, Ma—time I'm wasting now on bookkeeping. And it can't be learned down at the High School of Commerce."

He waited for his mother to say something, but as she remained silent he continued with increasing earnestness and heat. "Look, Ma, here's how I see it. I think I can be a success as a composer. I think I can be a *good* composer. But before I can do these things, I've got to go out and learn what popular music is all about."

"Popular songs—ragtime—that's not for a boy like you, George. If music makes you happier than bookkeeping, try to be someone important—like Mendelssohn."

"I *want* to be someone important—but I want to do it in my own way. I want to be an *American* Mendelssohn—a Mendelssohn of popular music."

"I don't know, George. I hear what you say. I turn it over in my mind. But it just doesn't make any sense to me. All I know is that a boy without education is a nothing. He can't amount to anything at all."

Eventually, however, Mother Gershwin gave

way, as George had known that she would. "Well, if you must do it," she told him, "I won't stop you. Papa won't like your giving up school, and I don't know how I'll explain it to him. But do what you think is best. How can I be sure that I am right and you are wrong?"

A friend interceded for Gershwin and procured an interview for him with the head of Remick's music-publishing house. After demonstrating his ability as a pianist, he asked for a post as staff pianist, and was accepted at a salary of fifteen dollars a week. Mamma Gershwin did not like her boy working as a hack pianist, and Papa grumbled at the fact that he had given up school. But to George, aged sixteen, his first position was very much of a personal triumph. He was now a cog in the machine of a nation's song business—not an important cog yet, but it was a beginning. Of that George was sure. He might be on the bottom step of his stairway to paradise. But nothing could now keep him from climbing to the top.

CHAPTER II

"Fascinating Rhythm . . ."

· *1* ·

TIN-PAN ALLEY, fabulous street of song, winds its way through the very heart of the American scene. In 1913, when George Gershwin first knew it, the section extended from Fifth to Sixth Avenues on 28th Street in midtown New York. But Tin-Pan Alley, though it acquired its name on 28th Street, had not originated there. It was born farther downtown, in gaslit Union Square. This part of the city had been, a generation before George's time, the home of grand opera in its proudest traditions; the old Academy of Music and Steinway Hall on 14th Street having been the center of the American opera and concert world until the building of the Metropolitan Opera House and Carnegie Hall. Then it gradually got taken over by nickelodeons, music-halls, and firms publishing popular music; and here the tunes of the nation were born. Witmark & Sons, leading song publishers, were in Union Square before 1890; Ted Snyder, too. Around these clustered lesser competitors who constantly struggled with one another in the mad scramble to create the song of the hour.

What created songs in Union Square was not inspiration, but mass production, competition, high-powered salesmanship, division of labor, song-plugging. These, rather than creative art, were responsible for the birth of hit songs. The Union Square music factory was a bedlam of noises: bands braying in practice sessions; tap-dancers trying out a new number to the rhythmic patter of toes; songsters and instrumentalists rehearsing new vaudeville routines; professional pianists banging out new tunes for possible clients—the music-hall managers, successful singers, and others through whose use the songs would be brought before the public and popularized. It must be borne in mind that these were the only methods possible thirty or forty years ago, before radio and phonograph records could be counted on to make a song popular all over the country and almost overnight. In that period, a song could become famous only after being sung or played by some prominent theatrical personality whose talent and charm helped to "put it over" until the public began to clamor for it.

In the bedlam that was Tin-Pan Alley, then, songs were manufactured with speed, precision, and efficiency. Formulas existed for every type of song, and dozens of weary troubadours, each with his own specialty, were on hand to produce music to these formulas. As the songs got written, they were rushed to the song-pluggers, whose duty it was to market them successfully to actors, jazz-bands, and theater managers.

For between each song and its success stood the influential figure of the song-plugger. Down at Union Square, as later in Tin-Pan Alley on 28th Street, the song-plugger was by far the most important factor in the music-publishing field. To the publisher, the composer was little more than an efficient piece-worker who could create a certain type of song on order at a given moment. The musical performer —the hack pianist who hammered out the tunes for clients—was a mere day laborer; hundreds of these pianists migrated from one publisher to another seeking employment. But the song-plugger—he was the artist of the trade. Whether a song caught on or "flopped" depended on his personality, talents, and salesmanship gifts. A good one could produce successes regardless of merit. There were not many really good song-pluggers like Pat Howley, for instance, and Meyer Cohen, who made a national sensation of "My Mother Was a Lady."

Every evening these song-pluggers, together with their competitors, assembled at Tony Pastor's Theatre, the city's leading music-hall. Pastor, who was tolerant of song-pluggers, allowed them to station themselves in different parts of his theater. A song sung on the stage—some example of a plugger's wares —would inspire a Pat Howley or a Meyer Cohen to rise from his seat (the limelight playing strongly on him) and sing the chorus until he felt that it was indelibly impressed on the audience's memory.

Another favorite haunt of the plugger was the large nickelodeons in Union Square, not yet called the "movies." Here were featured, as part of the cinema entertainment, song-slides with which the plugger could publicize his wares. Eddie Cantor, Georgie Jessel, and Walter Winchell entered the theater world, as children, by singing on the nickelodeon stage the tunes flashed on the screen by these slides.

When the evening show was over, the pluggers would gather at nearby beer-gardens to rub elbows

with actors, singers, and theater and nickelodeon managers. Cigars, drinks, lavish dinners were distributed
generously. During this burst of entertaining, the
plugger would ply his trade, spreading valuable publicity for his songs and trying to acquire clients.

By introducing the song-plugger into the song
industry, by making song-writing a highly specialized
business, Union Square paved the way for Tin-Pan
Alley. Tin-Pan Alley—or 28th Street—had its tra-
dition. It would soon create its own history.

· 2 ·

Early in 1898, Broder & Schlam, one of the most
prosperous of San Francisco's music-publishing firms,
moved to New York, opening on 28th Street—the
first of many rapid migrations to this street. Other
publishers wished to be where Broder & Schlam was;
for there, surely, would congregate the most famous
actors and managers seeking their songs. Next door
to Broder & Schlam moved Charles K. Harris, whose
fertile pen had created such sensational ballads as
"Break the News to Mother" and "After the Ball."
Other Union Square publishers followed Harris uptown. At 51 West 28th Street, Witmark & Sons established themselves; this firm published Victor Herbert, Ernest R. Ball, and numerous musical-comedy
successes, and was the leader in the business. Else-

where on 28th Street could now be found Harry Von Tilzer, his gaudy banners publicizing "Old New Hampshire Home"; Joseph Stern & Company, riding high on such successes as "The Little Lost Girl" and "Sweet Rosie O'Grady"; Leo Feist, then a novice among these veterans; and numerous other small firms.

The year 1898, therefore, converted 28th Street into the street of songs. All day long, pianos banged and trumpets blared the new numbers. Actors and musicians walked mechanically from one house to the next seeking fresh material. Because this street became so specialized, it soon acquired a name of its own. No one remembers certainly who was the first to christen it, though some say that it was a newspaper man named Monroe Rosenfeld who coined the name in a series of articles written for the *Herald* in or about 1903. But whoever did it had poetry in his veins. Tin-Pan Alley—no name could have been apter or more descriptive.

On 28th Street the song business developed to Gargantuan proportions. It became a huge machine, disgorging songs out of its busy mouth. And it was an efficient machine. Tin-Pan Alley separated songs into a number of categories: the humorous vaudeville ditty, the ballad, the love song, the ragtime melody, later the "blues" song, still later the "mammy" song. Each department boasted its special composers, and each its corps of expert musical stenographers to assist these composers in putting down their ideas on paper.

It was a highly sensitive and delicate mechanism that created song fashions and then produced songs to meet the fashions. Of this delicate mechanism the indispensable cog was still the song-plugger. He was easily recognizable, standing there in front of his employer's establishment, a cigar in his mouth, his derby slightly askew, his eye kept vigilantly on all passers-by. He had to know every important actor and musician by sight; the best of the song-pluggers knew them all intimately. Should an actor or a bandleader pass through Tin-Pan Alley, the song-plugger would do his best to entice him into the shop. Here he would work hard—utilizing the magnetism of his personality and the eloquence of cigars, theater tickets, dinners, bottles of whiskey—to convince his victim of the appeal of his new song-merchandise.

Once the song-plugger had induced the client to enter the publisher's office, the rest became routine— a routine in which Tin-Pan Alley was particularly efficient. The staff pianist hammered out a series of new tunes. Tap-dancers rapped out the rhythmic pattern. The sales department swore by the music's potential value as entertainment. The result of this routine was that the client would select the song or songs that particularly struck his fancy—and the rest now lay on the lap of chance.

· 3 ·

By the time George Gershwin entered Tin-Pan Alley, however, its sensitive mechanism was beginning to show signs of disintegration. Production of songs on an assembly belt was becoming less and less feasible. A new emphasis was being placed on subtlety of melody, rhythm, harmony. With this emphasis, the composer was rising to a status of new importance. As the writing of popular music grew somewhat more complicated, the old machinery— geared to turn out new songs by mass production—no longer functioned smoothly. Jazz, in short, was being born; and, by the same token, the Tin-Pan Alley of old was dying.

Popular music had undergone many changes of style in Tin-Pan Alley. In the 1890s the sentimental ballad was in vogue—sad, saccharine tunes for sad, saccharine lyrics. There were "After the Ball," "The Lost Child," "My Mother Was a Lady," "Sweet Adeline"—all of them expressions of a lush and sentimental era. When the song-writing business moved uptown from Union Square the vogue for the sentimental ballad was on the wane. A new style had come in—"ragtime," a syncopated rhythm born in New Orleans from Negro derivations and introduced in New

York by a pianist named Ben Harney at Tony Pastor's
Theatre in 1896. It caught on immediately and
spread like wildfire, for it was lively with the irresistible rhythm of dancing Negro feet; and it brought
new vitality, new energy, new pulse to the anemic
American song. The sentimental ballad had been
meant for singing; ragtime was meant for dancing,
and it set American toes to tingling!

But ragtime, even at its best, stood for ungovern-
able force, and jazz, which evolved from ragtime,
brought to it artistic discipline as well as design and
order. The derivation of the word *jazz* is to this day
a subject of controversy. Some derive the word from
the French *"jaser"*—meaning "to rattle" or "chat-
ter"; others say it is an outgrowth of a term familiar
in minstrel shows—"jasbo." Some say that the word is
Creole patois; while others believe that there must at
one time have been a dusky musician in the South
named Charles or James, and that the contraction of
his name ("Let's have some more of that music, *Chas*
—or *Jas!*") gave us the word.

If the origin of the word is obscure, however,
the musical ancestry of the type is clear. Jazz grew
out of the minstrel-show tune, the ragtime rhythm,
the Negro spiritual. It may be said to have been born
in or about 1913. At that time, Art Hickman introduced "sweet" music at the St. Francis Hotel in San

Francisco: more strings, less brass; more harmony, less rhythm. "Sweet" music was to bring a greater richness and variety of instrumentation to popular music; it was to introduce for the first time the art of arrangement. "Sweet" music was soon to find its high priest in Paul Whiteman. . . .

At about the same time when "sweet" music rose, W. C. Handy's "blues" also rose to popularity. The Negroid lament of the latter type was to give color and character to the contours of jazz's melodic line. Its original and—for popular music—strange harmonic construction was to become the spine and sinew of jazz: the "blues note," which harmony textbooks would identify as a flattened third or seventh; the "blues chord"—in harmonic vocabulary, an emphasis on subdominant harmonies and on seventh chords of the dominant. This was a far cry from the dull and stereotyped major triads formerly in general use by song-writers!

Jazz, in short, was sophisticated, stylized, even cultured ragtime. If the sentimental ballad was primarily for singing, and ragtime for dancing, jazz (in its highest form) was for *hearing*. It would bring subtlety and originality to the American popular song.

The year 1913—fateful for American music! Jazz is born. George Gershwin, going on sixteen, timidly enters Tin-Pan Alley as a professional pianist. Thus, quite coincidentally, jazz and Gershwin make their official appearance on the American song-scene simultaneously.

Thereafter, their fates were to be inextricably linked, for the story of jazz is, for the most part, the story of George Gershwin.

Music copyright by Harms, Inc.—used by permission

CHAPTER III

"Bidin' My Time . . ."

· 1 ·

AS proud of his new suit of clothes as of his job, sixteen-year-old George Gershwin took his place at Remick's. He was one of many assigned to private cubicles where they were made to hammer out tunes on the piano from morning to night. Clients came, crowded into the cubicles, listened to the songs, and took their pick.

The first feeling of excitement at belonging to Tin-Pan Alley and being a part of the feverish activity of song-writing soon gave way to boredom. George hated his work. He was expected to do his work automatically, to be a machine inside a still larger machine. Even at its best, playing the piano from morning till dusk, six days a week, was sickening drudgery. And piano-playing could hardly be at its best when its material was, with few exceptions, stereotyped and naïve—the work, generally, of illiterate musicians. George already had too fine a critical sense not to be impatient at the banal music he was called upon to play. One song was like the next—there was no imagination, no invention. Each composer seemed to have the same manner of turning a phrase or bringing about a cadence. "Why can't some of them learn to write a little differently for a change?" he would lament at home.

"You show them, George," his mother would say with conviction. "Some day they'll listen to you."

But the work at Remick's had value: as George had guessed instinctively, it proved to be a conservatory course in popular music. It taught him every phase of the song business from the inside. It brought him a highly sensitized and experienced approach to it. It taught him what was vulgar and what was good. As he played one song after another, day in, day out, he could dissect it part by part as a medical student dissects a frog. There was nothing in the anatomy of the popular song with which he was not soon familiar, no single trick whose secret he did not know. Most important of all, he learned all the formulas used by uninventive writers for various moods and emotions, and he realized at once that such useful formulas could never serve him in his own composition.

A less determined young man than George, less conscious of his own purpose, might have lost heart. What place had a sensitive and idealistic musician in the company of such mediocrity? But George never wavered for a moment in his self-appointed mission. And he never doubted himself or his aims. Greater intimacy with popular music did not altogether disabuse him of his belief in its ultimate artistic possibilities. On the contrary, his convictions were strengthened. Before his eyes, jazz was slowly taking form. George recognized that something important was happening to American music; that, with jazz, it was at last acquiring an independent style and idiom.

He had heard several songs—few and far between, of course—that made his heart sing with joy; they were so much like what he himself wanted to write! Among these were some by Irving Berlin— "Alexander's Ragtime Band," "Everybody's Doin' It," and "International Rag," for instance. As early as 1913 Irving Berlin was the leading figure in Tin-

Pan Alley. Like Gershwin's ancestors he had been born in Russia—in 1888. His background, also like George's, was the lower East Side to which he had been brought from the Old World in 1893, when he was five. He did not like school. Since theater blood rather than scholar's blood flowed in his veins, he ran away from home to become a "busker"—an entertainer on the sidewalks of New York. He also sang in saloons, working as a singing waiter at Coney Island, then at Nigger Mike's in Chinatown. In 1905, he went from door to door on 28th Street peddling his first song, "Marie from Sunny Italy"—for which, curiously enough, he had written the words, but *not* the music. Ted Snyder bought the song, which earned for its author a royalty of thirty-seven cents. His second song (for which he wrote the melody as well as the words) was "Dorando," also bought by Ted Snyder, this time for $25. Soon afterward he joined Ted Snyder's as a staff pianist, and from this moment became one of the best songpluggers in the business.

Berlin wrote one song after another, showing such originality and variety of style that Ted Snyder decided to take him as a partner in his publishing firm. It was not long before Berlin proved the wisdom of Snyder's move: in 1911, he wrote "Alexander's Ragtime Band," a song that took the country by storm. Berlin had hit his stride, and from now on he was to be one of the most productive, most highly gifted, and most successful song-writers in the country.

Irving Berlin had an endless fund of melodic ideas, ideas that sidestepped the stereotyped patterns employed by so many other popular composers. Irving Berlin could express sentiment without becoming maudlin, while in other songs he had rhythmic robustness. For these reasons, Gershwin—so often in despair at the unimaginative products of most Tin-Pan Alley composers—admired him profoundly. And Gershwin remained one of Berlin's most ardent admirers even after he himself joined Berlin as a leading American song-composer.

"Irving Berlin," Gershwin wrote after he had become world-famous, "was the first to free the American song from the nauseating sentimentality which had previously characterized it, and by introducing and perfecting ragtime he had actually given us the first germ of an American musical idiom.

"Irving Berlin is the greatest American song-composer. He has vitality, both rhythmic and melodic, which never seems to lose its freshness. He has that rich, colorful melodic flow which is ever the wonder of all those of us who, too, compose songs. His ideas are endless. His songs are exquisite cameos of perfection. Each one is as beautiful as its neighbor. Irving Berlin is America's Franz Schubert."

Still another composer delighted Gershwin with

his neatly turned melodies. Once, when George was a guest at his aunt's wedding at the Grand Central Hotel, the orchestra struck up a melody, and as George listened he grew tense with excitement. The subtle changes of tempo, the rich harmonization, the exciting originality of the melodic line stirred him. He listened spellbound. When the song was over, George rushed to the bandleader and asked for its title. It proved to be "You're Here and I'm Here," a number from a musical-comedy success called *The Girl from Utah,* and its composer was Jerome Kern. George begged the bandleader to play some other Kern melodies, and to each of them he listened breathlessly.

After that, Kern, like Berlin, became for Gershwin a model and an inspiration. With boyish adoration, he would stand in the street outside of Kern's house, hoping to hear him play the piano.

Kern was a son of New York City; he was born in 1885, thirteen years before George Gershwin. Hoping to make music his profession, he studied at the New York College of Music and with private teachers. His parents, however, insisted that he enter his father's business in New York, and Jerome had to yield. One of his first business deals (he was seventeen years old at the time) involved the purchase of two pianos. Always easily persuaded by soft words and an affable manner, he was sold by a glib salesman not two but two hundred pianos. After that, his father required no further convincing that the boy belonged to music and not to business.

Young Kern made a few trips to Europe, did some further study, and held a variety of jobs (both here and abroad) which brought him ever closer to his first love—popular music.   In New York, he got a job as pianist song-plugger with the Lyceum Publishing Company for $7 a week.   His duties consisted in playing the piano in the city's large department stores exploiting his publisher's lists.   In London, he found some work in the office of Charles Frohman, composing bits for the theater.

Then, in 1910, Kern was assigned to write the score for a New York show called *Mr. Wix of Wickham*—his first Broadway assignment.   He did an expert job and, in 1911, was commissioned to write his first original score for Broadway, *The Red Petticoat*. Three years later, in *The Girl from Utah*, he produced his first smash song-hit, a wistful tune sung by Julia Sanderson called "They Didn't Believe Me."   It was not long before he became known as one of the best musical-comedy composers.   Between 1915 and 1919 alone he was responsible for the music of at least nineteen productions.

"I studied Kern," Gershwin confessed many years later.   "I imitated him.   I admired him.   Many of the songs I wrote at the time sounded exactly like his."

· 2 ·

George was now writing songs in an uninterrupted creative flow. But it was some time before he
would find himself. In those early days he was obviously fumbling for a style of his own; as he himself
confessed, he imitated those whom he admired. It
was also some time before he was to get recognition.
But George did not permit failures to deflect him
from the goal he had set for himself. He would
create popular songs which a good musician could
listen to and respect, songs written with the meticulous
care and sincerity of an artist.

After all, he would often argue to himself,
had not even Mozart, Beethoven, Schubert, and
Brahms written so-called popular music: waltzes,
country dances, Ländler, Hungarian dances, in the
idiom best understood and assimilated by the masses?
Yet, because these composers approached popular
music with serious artistic purpose they wrote wonderful popular music. Had not Johann Strauss written
waltzes which were tremendous hits in their own day,
and yet none the less attained immortality? Why
could not a similar service be done for American popular music—for jazz?

"I regard jazz as an American folk music," he
wrote years later, expressing a lifelong conviction; "a

very powerful one which is probably in the blood of the American people more than any other style of folk music. I believe that it can be made the basis of serious symphonic works of lasting value."

"Jazz," he wrote again, "is music; it uses the same notes that Bach used. When jazz is played in another country it is called American. It is a very energetic kind of music, noisy, boisterous, and even vulgar. One thing is certain: jazz has contributed an enduring value to American achievement in the sense that it has expressed us. It is an original American achievement which will endure—not as jazz, perhaps —but which will leave its mark on future music in one form or another."

To make jazz an important musical idiom, George felt, was to be *his* mission. That there were composers like Jerome Kern and Irving Berlin on the scene, writing piquant and lovable melodies, convinced him that he was not dreaming idle dreams. He, too, would write unusual songs. . . .

Because he knew so clearly what he wanted to do— and knew it from the very first—he recognized neither discouragement nor obstacles. His ambition was a driving force before which he was helpless, a strong ocean current carrying him along in new directions. He was determined to succeed, and as a consequence he refused to believe that there were any closed doors which with will and patience he could not open.

He wanted, for example, to play his songs for Irving Berlin. The facts that Irving Berlin was one of the most successful composers in Tin-Pan Alley and that he, George Gershwin, was still a boy working in obscurity did not discourage him; he made the rounds of his acquaintances at Remick's until he found one who was willing to introduce him to the famous composer. Undisturbed at being, at last, in the presence of the man he admired so profoundly, George played a few of his songs for Berlin, and with quiet confidence talked of his aims and hopes. Berlin listened attentively and made no comment until George's musical and verbal recital was over. Then he put his arm around George's shoulder and told him that he had great talent.

"You are going to go very far, young fellow," Berlin said. "Just keep plugging."

That interview exhilarated George and fed his vanity. Even though it had no practical results— Berlin made no offer to get either publication or performance for any of Gershwin's songs—George felt that the meeting had been well worth while.

Other ventures, however, were not quite so satisfying. Sometimes while demonstrating songs for clients at Remick's he would surreptitiously include one of his own numbers. He kept hoping that some day someone would enter his cubicle, hear one of his songs, and—brushing aside all the others impatiently

—would single it out for praise and recognition. But the reality was unfortunately much more prosaic than George's daydreaming: his pieces went unnoticed, and presently he abandoned this stratagem.

He decided to submit his songs directly to the publishers. Naturally he would first try his own firm, Remick's. All the songs he submitted were turned down. Some were too sentimental, they said; others were not commercial enough.

"Look here, Gershwin," the manager at Remick's told him sharply; "you're here to play the piano —not to write songs. You'd better stick to your job, and let those who know how write the songs for us!"

George tried several other publishers, only to find them just as uninterested in his music. But failure was always just an incentive for George, and he kept on trying. Even as a child playing on the streets, he had never accepted defeat without a struggle. By the law of the streets the boy who could not take punishment was a coward; and George had never been accused of being a coward. Even now he could take punishment without whining, and come back fresh for more.

Eventually courage and determination must triumph—whether in street brawls or in life itself; and at last the miracle came to George. In 1916 one of his songs was accepted for publication by the house of Harry Von Tilzer—"When You Want 'Em You

Can't Get 'Em." From this, his first opus, George's earnings were exactly five dollars (the man who wrote the words got fifteen!). But the joy of officially entering the ranks of professional song-writers was greater reward than money. He handled the printed copy of his song with the loving devotion of a proud parent touching his first-born. He had arrived; he was a composer; a publisher had printed a song of his!

Now that the first hurdle had been leaped, George grew even more ambitious. He wanted to write music for the Broadway theater, just as Jerome Kern did. Once again he made contacts, pulled wires, tried every maneuver he could think of. For he had lately written a song that he believed would fit nicely into the show at the Winter Garden, home of lavish musical productions. And when presently he secured an interview with the managers of the Winter Garden shows, the two Shubert brothers, they were sufficiently impressed by the song to arrange a meeting between George and Sigmund Romberg, principal Winter Garden composer.

Romberg was encouraging—even flattering, and he went further: he offered to let George collaborate with him on the very next Winter Garden production, *The Passing Show of 1916*. As it turned out, George's part in this was but one song, "Making of a Girl"; but the occasion marked his emergence as a composer for the Broadway theater, and for this reason the meeting with Romberg proved a red-letter day both in Gershwin's career and in the history of the American musical comedy.

At about this time there came another opportunity for Gershwin to get one foot inside the doors, so to speak, of the Broadway theater. For it seemed that there was a job open for a rehearsal pianist for a show by Victor Herbert and Jerome Kern called *Miss 1917*. George applied for the job and got it. To work for Jerome Kern was naturally an exciting experience; but still more exciting was it for him to work in the theater itself—to be a part of what went on there, even if only an infinitesimal part. After a rehearsal was over, he would sit on, up on the stage, to look into the dark and empty auditorium and let his dreams soar. This was his second home; this was where he belonged; some day—soon!—he would be on a stage like this, but rehearsing his own music. . . .

The *Miss 1917* production included special Sunday evening concerts in which its star, Vivienne Segal, was the featured artist and George was the official accompanist. At one of these concerts Vivienne Segal sang two Gershwin songs—the first time that Gershwin songs had been heard at a professional performance. George was now nineteen years old, and another hurdle had been jumped.

It was not long after this that he had two of his songs published. Then several others were performed on Broadway. He began to feel that, in a certain modest fashion, he had won his spurs as a popular-song composer. And suddenly his cubicle at Remick's seemed too cramped for him and for his talent; he felt that if he stayed in it an hour longer he would stifle musically!

Obeying this impulse, then, he gave up his job, even though he knew that it would probably be some time before he could make any real money out of his music. But his emancipation from hack-work filled him with satisfaction and pride. His song-plugging days were over—from now on, he was a professional composer!

· 3 ·

Once the first exhilaration of freedom had waned, there came to George the sober consciousness that he still had to earn his living at tasks other than the writing of songs. He passed restlessly from one job to another, none of which proved any more attractive to him than had his grind at Remick's. He became a pianist at the City Theatre, a vaudeville house just off Union Square. His work was to consist in playing all the musical accompaniments during the supper hour when the orchestra was out for its evening meal. During his very first trial, however, he bungled the job badly, missing cues and sometimes playing altogether different music from what was being sung on the stage. The comedian bluntly made him the butt for impromptu humor, and the audience roared its laughter. George fled from the theater in the middle of the show, so ashamed of himself that he did not even have the courage to ask for his day's salary.

Then, for a brief period, he was the piano accompanist for Louise Dresser during her vaudeville tour; but this work merely bored the young and groping composer eager to make his mark with his own music.

One day, Irving Berlin—who had never forgotten the first impression that George made upon him—came to him with an attractive offer. Would George care to become his musical secretary? The salary was excellent, far more than George had earned in any of his other positions. The work was easy: all George had to do was to write down the melodies that Berlin dictated.

"The job is yours if you want it, George," Berlin told him. A moment later, a thoughtful expression came over Berlin's face, and he added: "However, much though I'd like to have you work for me, I hope you'll turn down the offer. You aren't meant to be my musical secretary—or anybody else's, for that matter. You have too much natural talent. This sort of job can only cramp your style. It might even rob you of your heaven-sent originality. You'll start imitating me, when it is much more important for you to remain yourself all the time. If you need the job and want it in spite of my advice, you can have it. But please, George, don't take it. You're meant for much bigger things. All you have to do is to keep on writing your songs, and be patient. Your day will come. I was never so sure of anything in my life!"

George revolved Berlin's words in his mind. The arguments for and against accepting the position sparred, like two agile boxers. He wanted a job; things weren't going well at home, and his salary was sadly needed; he didn't have a chance in the world of earning anywhere else even half as much as Berlin offered. On the other hand, Berlin said he had talent, and Berlin was convinced that the work might do him ultimate harm.

"All right, Mr. Berlin—you win," George said at last. "There's nothing I'd like better than to work for you. But if you advise me not to take the job, I won't."

"Now I'm *sure* you'll succeed, George!" Berlin exclaimed. "For I see you have guts as well as talent."

Suddenly, an unlooked-for opportunity came George's way. He was introduced to Max Dreyfus, head of the music-publishing house of Harms. Dreyfus, himself a composer, had flair—sensitive nostrils with which to smell out genius. It was Dreyfus who had discovered Jerome Kern; in later years he would also discover Richard Rodgers. Now, in the presence of nineteen-year-old George Gershwin, Dreyfus's nostrils once again began to quiver. Gershwin had published only two songs up to this time, songs with a certain charm, but hardly prophetic of the greatness to come. Yet Dreyfus recognized genius.

"You have good stuff in you, George," Dreyfus told him, "and I'll gamble on you, even if it takes years."

His offer was too good to be true: George was given $35 a week, without any set duties or regulated hours.

"All you have to do is to come around each day and say 'hello' to me," Dreyfus instructed George. "And keep composing. Show me what you're doing. I'm sure you'll make good."

George's career now began to unfold rapidly. A song of his, "You, Just You-oo," was taken for a musical-comedy success of 1918, *Hitchy-Koo*. Then he wrote "The Real American Folk Song," which was interpolated in another musical comedy of that year, *Ladies First*. The star of *Ladies First*, Nora Bayes, was impressed by George's talent and engaged him as her accompanist on a vaudeville tour. This partnership did not, however, prove a happy experience for either the star or her pianist. Nora Bayes wanted to sing one of Gershwin's songs, and she asked him to change the ending to make it more suitable for her voice. But George took his songs too seriously to re-vise them on order, and he stoutly refused.

"But, George, don't be foolish about it. My singing your song will go a long way towards making you famous. Other stars will want your songs, too."

"I'm sorry, Miss Bayes," George said emphati-cally; "I can't change a note of my song for you or for anyone."

"But even Irving Berlin once changed one of his songs for me! And, surely, you don't consider your-self a greater composer than Irving Berlin."

"No, of course I'm not 'greater than Irving Ber-lin'! But I can't change an ending to one of my songs on order. I just can't do it!"

Nora Bayes made a harsh comment; George countered with a vituperative reply—and they parted company.

Other Gershwin songs gradually made their way into theatrical productions. At last, through Max Dreyfus's influence, George was commissioned to write all the music for a Broadway revue, *Half-Past Eight*, but it was a dismal failure. The first show of Gersh-win's that may be called successful was *La La Lucille* in 1919.

A young producer named Alex Aarons was so convinced of George's talent that he commissioned him to write a musical-comedy score. (Later, it was

to be this producer who, in collaboration with Vinton
Freedley, brought out some of the biggest Gershwin
successes.) Here was the most ambitious assignment
that Gershwin had yet had, and it called for his best
efforts. The result was *La La Lucille*. After successful preliminary tryouts in Atlantic City and Boston,
the show opened in New York at the Henry Miller
Theatre on June 30, 1919. Here it ran for a half-
year, being very well received, owing almost entirely
to its gay and sprightly music; the hit song was "Nobody But You."

During the same year George wrote a song called
"Swanee," which was introduced at the Capitol Theatre in New York and which went unnoticed. It was
not a particularly distinguished song—not even up to
George's best standards at that time. But it boasted

Swan - ee,   How I love you, How I love you

a pleasing rhythmic pattern (conceived atop a Riverside Drive bus) and a rather fluent melody.* Compared with some of the songs of the hour (*Dardanella*
was the current sensation) it had originality and appeal. The next year Al Jolson heard it, bought it for
his show *Sinbad*—and promptly converted into a re-

* Music copyright by Harms, Inc.—used by permission.

sounding success a song that had begun as a failure. "Swanee" was sung from one end of the country to the other. Millions of copies of the sheet music and records were sold. In a few months George earned more money than he had ever before in his life seen at one time. There was no longer any necessity for him to fill unpleasant jobs. He could now devote himself exclusively to his composition.

George had produced his first hit. He was successful by the standards of Tin-Pan Alley. But by his own standards he knew that he still had far to go.

Bidin' My Time

Gracefully

I'm bid-in' my time; 'Cause that's the kind-a guy I'm

Music copyright by Harms, Inc.—used by permission.

CHAPTER IV

"Do It Again . . ."

· 1 ·

THE year in which George Gershwin emerged as a successful song-composer, 1919, was also the beginning of a fabulous era in America. The First World War had come to an end on a hysterical note: On November 11, 1918, the Armistice had been riotously celebrated in our streets with tears and shouts and embraces, with the banging of pots and pans, the tooting of raucous horns, and the spraying of confetti and torn-up newspapers and telephone books. The hysteria did not end that day, either, but persisted throughout the next decade.

Post-war readjustment caused upheavals in the social life of the country. Some of our fighting men returned from Europe with a tendency to set a low value on human life; and the consequence was that the post-war era was an era of murders, gang wars, and the rule of the gun by ruthless racketeers. Others returned with a fatalistic philosophy—"Today we're here, tomorrow we're gone!"—and so it was also an era of lavish parties, alcoholism, the feverish pursuit of good times, and the desire to make every passing moment count. Still others returned disillusioned with the attempt to "make the world safe for democracy"; and it became an era of cynical excesses and the rejection of all noble ideals.

The "roaring twenties" were tense and raucous, filled with strange emancipations, hollow emotions, and false attitudes. Beneath the cloak of sophistication many tried to hide their real feelings. Dancing flaunted new abandon in the "Charleston" and the "Black Bottom." Musical comedies and motion pictures grew more emphatic in their glorification of pleasure, and popular music frequently sounded a hysterical note.

A new conception of freedom was set up, and under its banner women began to march to liberation from old tabus and prejudices. Skirts grew shorter. Hair was bobbed. Cosmetics came into general use. Silk stockings, once restricted to the rich, were now considered every woman's right. Woman began to smoke in public, open sign of her emancipation. In 1920 she had acquired the right to vote; during the next few years she fought also for her right to full equality with man. She rid herself of many of her traditional obligations. As she grew impatient with housework, apartments replaced private homes, and mechanical accessories were considered indispensable. Sales of canned goods increased, and delicatessen stores more than doubled in number as substitutes were sought for the elaborate cooked meal.

The Volstead Act banishing the use of hard liquors—passed during the Spartan days of the war, and coming into force after the Armistice—had been designed to secure prohibition; actually it proved to lead to greater license. It created the speakeasy (where the younger generation spoke of itself as a "lost" generation), the hip-flask, the rum-running racketeer. Alcoholism spread behind closed doors as it had never before done in the open. Lawlessness was rampant. Political scandals in Washington—the "Teapot Dome" affair, for instance—further diminished popular respect for the law.

Sensationalism became a fetish. The public's appetite for spectacular murders was constantly whetted by the lurid journalism of the tabloids, an offspring of this decade. Magazines with fabulous circulations went in for gaudy material of a sensational character. Clara Bow discovered *It*, and Rudolph Valentino publicized male sex-appeal. The Bathing Beauty now came into prominence. The world of sport made heroes of Babe Ruth, Jack Dempsey, and Red Grange; for even in sports the hunt was tireless after new and more thrilling sensations.

The era was speed-crazy. In 1919, the average speed of an automobile on the road was 30 miles an hour; ten years later it was twice that. From 7,000,-000 registered passenger cars in 1919, the number swelled to 23,000,000 ten years later. The Twentieth Century Limited brought the speed of trains up to a mile a minute. Airplanes were also coming into more general use; and, in 1927, Charles A. Lindbergh made himself a popular idol by crossing the Atlantic Ocean alone in *The Spirit of St. Louis*.

Faddism was rampant. Coué was acclaimed for his theory of autosuggestion; then forgotten. Mahjong came into fashion. The crossword puzzle became a national pastime. Knowledge was swallowed in capsule form: an *Outline of History*, a *Story of Mankind*, a *Story of Philosophy*, and an *Outline of Science* became best-sellers; and one writer even went so far as to try to compress all human knowledge into a single volume!

It was also an age of expansion. The motion picture grew into a mighty industry, and toward the end of the decade it acquired a voice. The radio, originally regarded as hardly more than a curiosity, was proving to be one of the greatest scientific contributions of all time. Machines dominated life as never before. Skyscrapers were rising to new dizzy heights: the Empire State Building in New York City, erected during the closing years of the decade, towered more than a hundred stories high. Big business was growing fat with prosperity. America was a land of millionaires ("a chicken in every pot; a car in every garage"). The stock-market spiraled to unheard-of peaks as the entire nation gambled: in 1919, million-and-a-half-share days were considered unusual; ten years later, sixteen-million-share days were an every-day occurrence. In Florida, a phenomenal boom, one of many in different parts of the country, sent land prices to stratosphere levels.

Literature and the theater reflected the mood of the times. Style was racy, temper high-pitched. There was no effort at restraint. Novels like F. Scott Fitzgerald's *This Side of Paradise*, plays like *Chicago* and *What Price Glory?*, poetry like that of e. e. cummings, sophisticated verse by Dorothy Parker and Samuel Hoffenstein—all spoke for the era. Debunking was the attitude of the intellectual: Sinclair Lewis unmasked Main Street and Babbitt; H. L. Mencken and George Jean Nathan, the petty foibles of "boobus Americanus."

Then came a blue Monday at the end of October in 1929. The bubble that had grown to Gargantuan size suddenly burst. The stock market crashed—and with that crash an era fell into ruins. Millionaires became paupers overnight. Coolidge prosperity gave way to Hoover depression. The panic that followed had a sobering effect on an inebriated generation; it was the "hangover" after the period of revelry. The mad dance in which the decade had been spinning came to an abrupt halt.

It was during this feverish epoch that George Gershwin rose to national prominence. And one of the reasons he became so famous was that in his music the epoch found its reflection.

· 2 ·

Once he had become the proud father of such a hit as "Swanee," Gershwin found that, at last, permanent success was his. He was no longer a novice knocking at doors that refused to open. He was now accepted as a full-fledged son of Tin-Pan Alley and was eagerly sought out for new songs. The prominent producer George White engaged Gershwin to write the music for the 1920 edition of his annual revue, *George White's Scandals*. This revue was, every season, among the most lavishly presented musical shows on Broadway; that George was asked to write its music meant that he had "arrived." For the *Scandals of 1920* he wrote "Idle Dreams," "My Lady," "The Songs of Long Ago," and others that helped to establish his growing reputation.

In addition, the producer of a musical comedy called *A Dangerous Maid* asked him for six special numbers for it; among these were "Dancing Shoes," "Boy Wanted," "Some Rain Must Fall," and "Simple Life." Other productions, too, demanded feature songs from him; so that it was not long before Gershwin songs—sometimes one, sometimes several—were heard in more than a half-dozen Broadway shows within a short period. Two of these starred Ed Wynn, and one starred Irene Bordoni. And soon there even came to him an assignment from London! Only recently past his twenty-first birthday, George had already found his niche.

With George's increasing good fortune, the Gershwin family moved westward and uptown to a large apartment at 110th Street and Amsterdam Avenue. The activity of the entire household now revolved around him. Papa Gershwin could hardly believe that it was George who was the big wage-earner for the family. And through music! He regarded his son's rising fame with incredulity and skepticism, almost as if it were some fantastic dream from which he must surely awaken. Mamma Gershwin found endless pleasure in telling her neighbors how as a boy George had been convinced of his ultimate success. "Can you imagine?" she would say repeatedly. "We wanted him all the time to become a bookkeeper!"

As George's success grew, his home assumed more and more the populous activity of a railroad station. At the apartment on Amsterdam Avenue—as later in his private home on 103rd Street near Riverside Drive—there were always people about, from early afternoon until late at night. Neighbors, relatives, friends—sometimes even casual acquaintances and strangers—roamed freely around in the Gershwin home to bask in the sunshine of George's fame. They gathered in small groups in the different rooms. They played billiards, drank tea, talked. In his studio they clustered around his piano, watching him as he worked; and he did not always know who they were. The noise and the confusion were often too much even for him, and—knee-deep in some important assignment—he would have to escape for a few days to rooms in a nearby hotel. But when the immediate job was done, he always returned eagerly to his own setting, for he loved the crowds, the confusion, the society of people.

Not that success had transformed George into a

temperamental musician—far from it! Recognition, as a matter of fact, brought about little change in him. He was still the earnest, self-critical young musician determined to seek out new worlds. The quiet and unassuming modesty that was one of his most charming traits throughout his life enabled him to adopt a healthy attitude towards his own career. What he had done was so little compared with what he hoped to do! How, then, could he indulge himself in complacency? But success is a heady wine, and Gershwin was normal enough to have his moments of intoxication. He liked to talk endlessly about his work, his assignments, his hopes; about the wonderful reviews he received; about the kind words that were said about him by people in high places. He liked to take his own music apart for interested admirers and show them what he was trying to do that was *different*. He liked playing his own songs. But, to balance this intoxication, there were sober moments as well, and in such moments he saw with clarity that he had to work hard if he was ever to reach his goal.

And he worked hard. Success could never tempt him into adopting some pliable and practical formula for his songs. He was striving for a melody with mobility, a melody fluent and spontaneous, that would avoid the usual structural clichés. Such a melody could come only after the most painstaking carving and editing. He slaved over his rhythmic effects; he wanted them to be glib, subtle, cogent. He sweated to make his harmonic language rich and original; not for him the formulistic tonic-dominant chords of the Tin-Pan Alley composer. Many songs were temporarily discarded, not to be picked up again for several years. Others were permanently destroyed. For every one that saw the light of day, a dozen were scrapped.

Gradually he was giving shape and form to his musical speech. His first songs, though catchy, were set tunes to a set design. He wanted an idiom that was both catchy *and* original, and he achieved this through the sweat and tears of hard work: endless experiments at the piano, indefatigable trial and error with pencil and paper. Intuition was not enough for his purposes; not even his wonderful talent sufficed, though it was a talent that caused melodic ideas to burst from him in an almost uninterrupted geyser flow. He had had only a haphazard musical training. What rules and lessons would not bring to his fingertips, experience would.

Then, at last, there they were—the first Gershwin songs with a language, a style, an enchantment all their own. These songs led jazz to sophistication and maturity. No one else in Tin-Pan Alley—no, not even Irving Berlin nor Jerome Kern—wrote songs with so individual a flavor, so high a degree of technical ingenuity. "I'll Build a Stairway to Paradise"

was written for the *Scandals of 1922;* "Do It Again,"
in Irene Bordoni's success *The French Doll,* also belongs to 1922. Two years later came still more captivating examples of Gershwin's song-art: "Somebody
Loves Me" * from the *Scandals of 1924,* and "Oh,
Lady, Be Good" from the musical comedy *Lady, Be
Good.*

Some-bod-y   loves me,   I won-der   who,

There could be no question that George was
sounding a new note in American popular music.
These were fascinating tunes he was creating, tunes
whose appeal was heightened with repeated hearings.
Beyond their melodic charm, moreover, they revealed
extraordinary compositorial skill: now a modulation,
achieved with wonderful simplicity and inevitability,
produced a poignant effect; now the subtle and ca-
ressing play of the intricate rhythms achieved a dynamic quality; now the flavor of the harmonic language brought piquancy and spice. Occasionally, as
in "Do It Again," George's touch is light and infectious. Sometimes, as in "I'll Build a Stairway to
Paradise," his idiom is suave and elegant. Frequently, the style has aristocratic dignity, as in the

* Music copyright by Harms, Inc.—used by permission.

iyric flow of "Somebody Loves Me." In certain songs, like "Oh, Lady, Be Good," the drive is irresistible. Already Gershwin was proving himself a master of many different moods and styles. In the early 1920s, he made Broadway rub its ears with incredulity—Broadway had never believed that jazz could sound this way!

Besides finding himself, George had now discovered the ideal collaborator to supply lyrics for his songs. Like the Blue Bird of the Maeterlinck fantasy, this collaborator was found at home. . . .

Ira Gershwin had been dabbling with the pen for some time before he began working with George. At the College of the City of New York he contributed pieces to the college periodicals. He was, indeed, more successful as a writer than as a student. In spite of Mamma Gershwin's wishes, Ira was no scholar. He failed in his courses at the college and was transferred to the evening session. He entered Columbia Extension for pre-medical study, but was dropped six months later. Then he tried to take the course leading to examinations for teaching positions, but here again he failed.

At this point Ira decided to try authorship, this ambition having been fed when a squib of his had been bought—for a dollar!—by the editors of the Smart Set, H. L. Mencken and George Jean Nathan. But while waiting for a literary career to materialize, he had to find a job, and he got one with a traveling circus. It was while he was on this job that he turned his hand for the first time to the writing of lyrics— verses to be set to music—inspired, no doubt, by his brother's rising star as a composer.

It was in 1918 that the two Gershwins wrote their first song together—the one mentioned in Chapter III, "The Real American Folk Song," featured by Nora Bayes in *Ladies First*. Measured by the standards of the time it was a good lyric—fleet, neatly turned, witty. There followed some other collaborations with George, the most successful being "I'll Build a Stairway to Paradise" (*Scandals of 1922*). At the same time, Ira wrote a few lyrics for other popular composers of the day. All this was a valuable apprenticeship for Ira, who soon became a master of the craft.

In 1924, the Gershwin brothers wrote their first complete show, *Lady, Be Good*—an outstanding success. Thenceforth the song partnership of George and Ira Gershwin remained intact until George's death. Each inspired the other; each drew strength from the other. George's musical subtlety inspired Ira to produce lyrics which, at their best, were incomparable for deftness of touch; and Ira's lyrics frequently inspired George to write his best melodies. . . .

· 3 ·

Others besides Max Dreyfus and Irving Berlin realized that George Gershwin was revolutionizing the popular song. Soon after *La La Lucille* was produced, a famous composer of operettas, Victor Jacobi, stopped George at his publisher's and told him how much he liked his music. "You are miles ahead of all of us," Jacobi said. Jerome Kern, too, was enthusiastic in his praises of the young composer.

Even outside of Tin-Pan Alley there were those who remarked George's wonderful gifts. As early as September 1922 the American composer and pianist Beryl Rubinstein, in a newspaper interview, called Gershwin a "great composer." When the interviewer seemed amused by the thought of applying the adjective "great" to a composer of popular songs, Rubinstein added warmly: "I am absolutely in earnest. . . . This young fellow . . . has the spark of musical genius which is definite in his serious moods."

Then, with extraordinary insight and perception, Rubinstein went on to say:

"With Gershwin's style and seriousness he is not definitely of the popular-music school, but is one of the really outstanding figures in this country's serious musical efforts. . . . This young man has great charm and a most magnetic personality, and I really believe that America will at no distant date honor him for his talent . . . and that when we speak of American composers George Gershwin's name will be prominent on our list."

Mark the year of this interview—1922! Jazz was still a stepchild of music, disreputable, held in contempt. Gershwin was but twenty-four, and his *Rhapsody in Blue*—which was to reveal his full creative powers—was yet to be written. For Beryl Rubinstein to let such a statement reach publication required courage and conviction on the part of a serious musician!

Another of George's early sponsors, the famous concert singer Eva Gauthier, expressed her enthusiasm in concrete and dramatic form. In a recital in Aeolian Hall, New York, on November 1, 1923, Mme Gauthier sang works by such important modern composers as Bartók, Schönberg, Milhaud, and Hindemith, and by such old masters as Byrd, Purcell, and Bellini. One of her song-groups was—with remarkable courage and independence—devoted to jazz. In this group she included a song by Irving Berlin, another by Jerome Kern, and three by Gershwin: "I'll Build a Stairway to Paradise," "Innocent Ingenue Baby," and "Swanee"; and a fourth Gershwin song, "Do It Again," was sung as an encore. George himself was the accompanist for the entire jazz group. The event marked the first entry of jazz into the austere and sedate halls of concert music, and it was led there—appropriately—by the hand of George Gershwin.

"I consider this one of the very most important events in musical history," wrote the novelist Carl Van Vechten to a friend, and he ventured what proved to be a felicitous stroke of prophecy: "I suggest that we get up a torchlight procession headed by Paul Whiteman and his orchestra to honor Miss Gauthier, the pioneer. Mind you, I prophesy that the Philharmonic will be doing it within two years." And in exactly two years, the New York Symphony Society Orchestra presented the world première of Gershwin's jazz piano concerto!

Deems Taylor, then the music critic of the New York *World*, acknowledged that the Gauthier concert was an event of artistic importance. "It seemed to one listener," he wrote in his column, "that the jazz numbers stood up amazingly well, not only as entertainment but as music. . . . What they did possess was melodic interest and continuity, harmonic appropriateness, well-balanced, almost classically severe form, and subtle and fascinating rhythm—in short the qualities that any sincere and interesting music possesses."

This was the first time that a serious and significant music critic had considered jazz of enough importance to be subjected to the same critical scrutiny and analysis that he would give to a symphony or a concerto. For jazz, emancipation was now just around the corner. . . .

One of the first to congratulate George after the Gauthier concert was Paul Whiteman, the same Paul Whiteman whom Carl Van Vechten had named to lead the torchlight parade for the singer. Whiteman, recently crowned by newspapermen "King of Jazz," shook hands vigorously with jazz's Crown Prince. "You were wonderful, George, and your music is wonderful! Why don't you write a large work for my orchestra? If it's as good as your songs, I'll even hire Carnegie Hall and play it there."

George laughed his abrupt, nervous laugh. "And if you pack Carnegie Hall to the doors, Paul, you may be sure it won't be my music that will be doing it, but your wonderful orchestra."

Paul Whiteman and George Gershwin had met some years before the Gauthier concert. A graduate from symphony orchestras (he had played the viola in symphonic organizations in Denver and San Francisco), Whiteman had made his debut as conductor during the First World War when he led a forty-piece band. After the War, he organized an orchestra of his own which played in Santa Barbara, California; and so the Paul Whiteman Orchestra was born.

Like Gershwin, Whiteman had entered the field

of popular music determined to open up new artistic horizons for it. What concerned him, as a conductor, was the elevation of the style of jazz performance. He believed that for too long a time jazz music had been subjected to haphazard and slipshod playing at the hands of incompetent musicians, and that—instead—it ought to be as carefully rehearsed as symphonic music. He was determined to entrust jazz orchestrations to skilled technicians only. (It was Whiteman, incidentally, who officially introduced the art of arranging.) He believed in "sweet music"—most jazz bands at the time were too raucous for his taste. "Symphonic jazz" came into vogue with Whiteman; and Whiteman came into vogue with symphonic jazz.

Whiteman's success was meteoric. At the Alexandria Hotel in Los Angeles he attracted the attention of the entire West Coast to the soft, rich strains of his music. Then, coming east to New York, he created a sensation at the Ambassador Hotel and at the Palais Royal night club. In 1923 he toured Europe, and his tour was a succession of triumphs. His new way of playing popular music—a new way that consisted merely in playing it as if it were serious music—made him the leading jazz performer in the world; just as Gershwin's new way of writing popular music was rapidly making him its leading composer.

Inevitably, the trails of jazz's leading performer and of its leading composer must meet. Whiteman had often played Gershwin melodies, re-dressed in new orchestrations provided by Whiteman's ace arranger, Ferde Grofé. Whiteman knew at once that here was a composer who thought along his own lines —who knew, just as Whiteman knew, that jazz was destined for a place of honor under the musical sun. Whiteman may have guessed that their trails, now meeting for the first time, would soon join to form the broad and magnificent highway of great popular music.

Whiteman soon had stronger indications that his faith in the young composer had not been misplaced. There was Gershwin's ever-increasing astuteness and fertility as a composer of songs. But, curiously enough, it was not a Gershwin success, but a Gershwin failure, that convinced Whiteman of the young man's genius.

In 1923, Paul Whiteman and his orchestra were featured in the George White *Scandals*. One of the compositions they were asked to play was an experimental one-act Negro opera called *135th Street*, book by De Sylva, music by Gershwin. Into this one-act opera (precursor of the later and greater *Porgy and Bess*) Gershwin poured some of his happiest inspiration up to that time. As Paul Whiteman rehearsed his orchestra in the score, he was convinced that here

was the first genuinely important attempt at the creation of native American opera. George White also
was enthusiastic. The theme of the opera was som-
ber, the action ending with murder. The setting was
drab: a basement café near 135th Street and Lenox
Avenue. But Gershwin's wonderful lyric vein
gushed, pouring forth the warm blood of his melodies. After a tryout performance in New Haven,
one critic went so far as to write that "this opera will
be imitated in a hundred years." At the New York
opening of the *Scandals of 1923* opinion was divided:
some considered it hopelessly bad and pretentious,
whereas others thought that it opened new horizons
for jazz music.

After a single performance, George White had
a change of heart about the opera. He still liked the
music and was convinced that the work had artistic
merits; but he also felt, on second thought, that it
had no place in a Broadway revue—it was too morbid,
it cast a melancholy pall over the numbers that followed. For the sake of the show as a whole, therefore, he decided to drop it altogether. Thus Gershwin's little opera had had only one performance
(though it was to be repeated a few years later at
Carnegie Hall at a Paul Whiteman concert); and, in
spite of some kind criticisms, it was a failure.

But Whiteman had never forgotten it. He knew
that as an artistic work it had glaring faults. It

boasted some wonderful melodies, but they were not always well knit together. At many moments the music faltered, without definite direction or purpose. But Whiteman realized also that here was a native expression, bringing to opera an American flavor it had never before had; and, more than anything else, it proved to him that Gershwin was meant for achievements in fields more spacious than that of the popular song, that if Gershwin ever ventured into symphony, opera, or concerto he might produce great and imperishable music.

When, therefore, Whiteman first broached to Gershwin the suggestion that he write a large work for him, he was expressing what for some time had assumed real importance in his mind. He believed that jazz already had gone a considerable distance towards its emancipation as music. Now he was tempted to put jazz to the acid test: to present a concert of jazz music in a serious New York concert hall before a serious musical audience. He wanted jazz to stand or to fall as a serious musical product. For such a concert, Whiteman wanted a large symphonic work in the jazz idiom—the final, convincing proof that jazz had grown up to maturity. And who was better equipped to compose such a large work than young Gershwin, who had already demonstrated what could be done in that vein with his one-act opera?

"What do you say, George?" Whiteman would

ask him from time to time. "When will you sit down and write for me a great piece of music, such as only you are capable of doing?"

But Gershwin took the suggestion lightly. He was in no mood for serious composition. For one thing, he was ever conscious of his musical shortcomings. He knew enough about music to realize that he knew too little. How could he, with his lamentable technique and his inadequate musical education, possibly write a large work for symphony orchestra?

"Why do you come to *me*, Paul?" Gershwin asked, when once he realized that Whiteman was serious. "I wouldn't know how to write a big work if my life depended on it. There are so many gifted composers around in New York who could shake such a work out of their sleeves. They are trained for such a job—I'm not. Their contribution would do credit to your concert—mine wouldn't. No, Paul, I'd better stick to my songs."

"George, if you'd only try, you make the other American composers ashamed of themselves—with all their studies and training! It's your music I want for my concert, not theirs. Your music would be fresh and inspired. Theirs would only be manufactured."

"No—it just won't do, Paul. Besides, I haven't the time now to sit down and work at an important

piece of music. Right now I have contracts to pro‹
vide songs for no fewer than four musical comedies,
all for early production. Even if I wanted to listen
to your crazy scheme, I couldn't find the time for it.
Some day, perhaps. . . ."

Music copyright by Harms, Inc.—used by permission

CHAPTER V

" 'S Wonderful . . ."

· 1 ·

THAT day came sooner than George expected. He was reading the New York *Tribune* one morning when a publicity notice caught his eye. It announced a jazz concert by Paul Whiteman and his orchestra at Aeolian Hall, and one line made George's heart stand still. He reread it twice to make sure that it was no hallucination. What he read was that the major work on the program was to be a new and large symphonic-jazz work by George Gershwin.

A large work for orchestra was, at the moment, far from George's thoughts. He had not promised any to Whiteman; indeed, he had repeatedly told Whiteman that he was unprepared to undertake such an assignment. He reached for the telephone and asked Whiteman for an explanation.

"Look, George," Whiteman said pleadingly. "I know it comes as a surprise to you. But I'm in a hole and you're the only one who can help me. I've got an awfully big stake in this concert. I'm out to show the world that jazz is something important and original in music. If I fail, George, I'll be the laughingstock of the music business. That's the chance I'm taking, but I think it's worth the gamble."

"I know, Paul, and I sympathize with you," said George. "But I can't write a large work on short notice as if it were just another song. Man alive, I've never written a large symphonic work before, and here you go expecting me to do it in three weeks!"

"You have it in you, George, and you can do it. With your talent you can do it in three weeks. Without that talent you couldn't do it in three years. Come now, George, be a sport about it. If I don't have a big work as the center of interest for my concert it will be a bust, and you know it. You're the only guy who can compose such a work—at least, you're the only guy *I* want to have compose such a work. Be a good fellow. Do it for my sake. Do it for your own sake, and for the sake of your artistic conscience. Do it for the sake of jazz. With your talent, George, you'll make history."

The irresistible flow of Whiteman's arguments was too persuasive to be dismissed, and George found himself promising Whiteman that he would write the work—or, at least, would try his best.

"That's all I'm asking, George," Whiteman said jubilantly, "that you should try your best."

One moment after he put the telephone receiver back on its hook, George cursed his stupidity in acceding to Whiteman. That concert was announced for February 12—he had only a few weeks! He had never in his life written anything larger than a song; his one-act opera had been, after all, only a combination of several songs. He didn't have a single idea in his head. Worst of all, he felt that his technique was not equal to so formidable an undertaking. He would surely make a mess of it—bring ridicule on Whiteman's head and on his own. He had no right to accept a job that was beyond his capabilities. . . . Then—

"Suddenly an idea occurred to me," he said later. "There had been so much talk about the limitations of jazz, not to speak of the manifest misunderstanding of its function. Jazz, they said, had to be in strict time. It had to cling to dance rhythms. I resolved, if possible, to kill that misconception with one sturdy blow. Inspired by this aim, I set to work composing.

"I had no set plan, no structure to which my music could conform. The Rhapsody, you see, began as a purpose, not a plan. I worked out a few themes, but just at this time I had to appear in Boston for the première of *Sweet Little Devil*. It was on the train, with its steely rhythms, its rattly-bang that is so often stimulating to a composer (I frequently hear music in the very heart of noise), that I suddenly heard—even saw on paper—the complete construction of the Rhapsody from beginning to end. No new themes came to me, but I worked on the thematic material already in my mind, and tried to conceive the composition as a whole. I hear it as a sort of musical kaleidoscope of America—of our vast melting-pot, of our incomparable national pep, our blues, our metropolitan madness. By the time I reached Boston, I had the definite plot of the piece, as distinguished from its actual substance.

"The middle theme came upon me suddenly, as my music often does. It was at the home of a friend, just after I got back to Gotham. I must do a great deal of what you might call subconscious composing, and this is an example. Playing at parties is one of my notorious weaknesses. As I was playing, without a thought of the Rhapsody, all at once I heard myself playing a theme that must have been haunting me inside, seeking outlet. No sooner had it oozed out of my fingers than I realized I had found it. Within a week of my return from Boston I had completed the structure, in the rough, of the *Rhapsody in Blue*."

George worked hard on the revision of his ambitious work. He was too self-critical to be easily satisfied. Frantically, Whiteman begged for the manuscript; just as frantically, George insisted that he needed more time for polishing its rough surfaces.

One problem after another had to be solved. For example, there was the very opening of the composition. George knew what he wanted. He had a theme in mind that would set off the entire work as a spark sets off a firecracker. It would be an ascending glissando for the clarinet—a nervous, raucous wail, which would at once establish the mood of abandon. He showed the theme to a few clarinetists and told them what he wanted. They said that no clarinetist in the world could play the passage in just that way, that it was beyond the technique of the clarinet. But George was stubborn, and would make no compromises.

Then he talked to Ross Gorman, clarinetist of the Whiteman orchestra. Gorman experimented for five days with different types of reeds—and then shouted "Eureka!"

Whiteman kept Gershwin's telephone ringing, and a steady stream of Western Union messengers going to Gershwin's house. He was indefatigable in his pleas that George finish his composition once and for all. The day of the concert was drawing menacingly near and Whiteman had not even begun rehearsing the work. But always Whiteman received the same cool answer: The composition needed more revision; there were still a few knotty problems that cried for a solution; not until the composer was satisfied would he permit it to leave his hands.

In Whiteman's heart there lurked the terrible fear that perhaps Gershwin would *never* surrender the work—that the concert would take place without benefit of a major composition. At last, in despair, Whiteman invaded Gershwin's study and swore that he would not leave until Gershwin gave him his word of honor that he would complete the manuscript within a few days. It was then that Gershwin decided, somewhat regretfully, to surrender the music. Sheet by sheet he passed it over to Whiteman, who rushed it to Ferde Grofé for orchestration, and from him it returned to Whiteman for rehearsal.

At the first full rehearsal of the *Rhapsody in Blue*, Whiteman was so absorbed in the music that at times he forgot that he was conducting. By the time the composition had reached its midway point, he no longer made any pretense of directing. Slipping his baton under his arm, he listened to the music with open ears, and with incredulity. He had expected

George to write an interesting work; but *this* was nothing short of genius! Then, when the saxophones and strings poured forth the beautiful lyric section— the section which Whiteman was henceforth to adopt as his identifying signature over the radio—Whiteman's stick fell from under his arm. He was trembling with excitement.

"Damn that fellow!" Whiteman said after this first rehearsal. "Did he actually think he could improve it?"

Soon afterward, Whiteman called a few music critics and professional musicians to the Palais Royal one morning to hear the final rehearsal of the *Rhapsody*. This night club, which only a few hours earlier had disgorged its last customers, was in a state of undress; the chairs were piled on the bare tables, and women were mopping the floors. Whiteman and his men contributed to the informality of the setting. They were all in shirt sleeves, some of them were smoking, others were chatting amiably. Whiteman, in a sweater, and Gershwin, in his vest, were at the piano studying the manuscript.

"I've got hold of something that you might sharpen your teeth on," Whiteman told the critic, Leonard Liebling. "And I don't mean breakfast."

Before this small and select audience, the *Rhapsody* received its first performance. There were some expressions of praise. Others were frankly puzzled by the unorthodoxy of the musical idiom. At Gershwin's suggestion, the work was repeated. This time all doubts were dissipated: everybody agreed that Gershwin had composed an important work—though precisely how important it really was none of them could be expected to realize at that time.

At last the afternoon of the concert arrived— Lincoln's birthday, February 12, 1924, and a most appropriate day: for was not the *Rhapsody in Blue* the Emancipation Proclamation for a Negroid musical expression? The élite of the music world came to Aeolian Hall, attracted by so strange a curiosity as a concert of jazz music in a dignified concert hall. Not only the major music critics were present but also world-famous artists in every field of musical endeavor: Rachmaninoff, Godowsky, Mengelberg, Stravinsky, Stokowski, Victor Herbert, Damrosch, Heifetz, Elman, Kreisler, John Philip Sousa—these and many others.

"Fifteen minutes before the concert was to begin," Whiteman recalls, in his autobiography, "I yielded to a nervous longing to see for myself what was happening out front, and putting on an overcoat over my concert clothes, I slipped around to the entrance of Aeolian Hall.

"There I gazed upon a picture that should have imparted new vigor to my wilting confidence. It was snowing, but men and women were fighting to get into the door, pulling and mauling each other as they sometimes do at a baseball game, or a prize fight, or in the subway. Such was my state of mind at the time that I wondered if I had come to the right entrance. And then I saw Victor Herbert going in. It was the right entrance, sure enough, and the next day, the ticket-office people said they could have sold out the house ten times over.

"I went back stage again, more scared than ever. Black fear simply possessed me. I paced the floor, gnawed my thumbs, and vowed I'd give five thousand dollars if I could stop right then and there. Now that the audience had come, perhaps I had really nothing to offer them at all. I even made excuses to keep the curtain from rising on schedule. But finally there was no longer any way of postponing the evil moment. The curtain went up and before I could dash forth, as I was tempted to do, and announce that there wouldn't be any concert, we were in the midst of it."

The concert included a rich variety of popular songs old and new, good and bad, arranged in an intriguing formation. The first group contrasted the jazz of 1914 with that of 1924. A second group offered comedy numbers. A third directed attention to new jazz orchestrations. One set of pieces was made up of symphonic arrangements of jazz numbers, while another set comprised jazz arrangements of classical numbers.

The novelty of the music provided some interest. But before the program had progressed beyond the first few groups there were visible signs of boredom here and there in the auditorium. There was some mild applause, and some scattered interest. But restlessness was beginning to spread through the house— restlessness, and the feeling that the experiment, for all its novelty, was a "bust."

Then came Gershwin's *Rhapsody in Blue*—the tenth and penultimate number on the program. . . .

With the first whine of the clarinet, the audience pricked up its ears. Now, it was really interested. "Somewhere in the middle of the score," confessed Whiteman, "I began crying. When I came to myself, I was eleven pages along, and to this day I cannot tell you how I conducted that far."

The response to the *Rhapsody* was electric. The audience had never before heard music such as this. It guessed that something epochal had taken place, and it expressed its delight in an overwhelming demonstration of cheers and applause.

The critics the next morning were equally enthusiastic. "This composition," wrote Olin Downes, "shows extraordinary talent." Gilbert Gabriel remarked, "Mr. Gershwin has an irrepressible pack of talents, and there is an element of inevitability about the piece." William J. Henderson prophesied: "Mr. Gershwin will be heard from often, and one music lover who became an admirer of his art . . . earnestly hopes he will keep to the field in which he is a free and independent creator." Deems Taylor was of the opinion that the *Rhapsody* "reveals a genuine melodic gift and a piquant and individual harmonic sense to lend significance to its rhythmic ingenuity. Moreover, it is genuine jazz music, not only in its scoring, but in its idiom."

Some expressed their enthusiasm in even more extravagant language. Henry O. Osgood, an editor of the *Musical Courier*, believed that the *Rhapsody* "is a more important contribution to music than Stravinsky's *Rites of Spring*." And that venerable dean of New York music critics, Henry T. Finck, found Gershwin "far superior to Schönberg, Milhaud, and the rest of the futurist fellows."

Such enthusiasm proved only a breeze compared with the tempest that followed. The *Rhapsody in Blue* soon became the most famous American symphonic work, and its author one of the best-known and best-loved of living American composers. The sale of phonograph records and sheet music, and the performance royalties made Gershwin a rich man. The work has since been arranged for solo piano, for two pianos, for eight; for solo harmonica, for harmonica orchestra, for mandolin orchestra, and for chorus. When the screen acquired a voice it paid $50,000 for the right to include it in a musical-comedy extravaganza. Roxy's Theatre, then the leading cinema palace in New York, was reported to have paid $10,000 for the right to include it in a stage production for one week. It was adapted for ballet, and Jack Donahue used it as a tap dance. When Paul Whiteman began to conduct regularly on the air, he chose the lyric section as his radio signature. Most important of all, the *Rhapsody* became a permanent fixture in the repertory of American and European symphony orchestras, performed throughout the world as one of the foremost musical contributions of our country and our times. What was perhaps the final accolade of approval was bestowed on the *Rhapsody* when, on the afternoon of November 1, 1942, Arturo Toscanini conducted it over the radio for a nationwide audience.

Moreover, the *Rhapsody* brought to other American composers the realization that jazz was an important musical idiom, capable of being used successfully in large musical forms. Directly or indirectly it inspired John Alden Carpenter to write his ballet, *Skyscrapers*; Aaron Copland to write a jazz piano concerto; George Antheil to write a jazz opera, *Transatlantic*.

In Europe, too, the strains of the *Rhapsody* made a profound impression, inspiring Maurice Ravel to write a "blues." In Germany, Ernst Křenek and Kurt Weill were encouraged to write their famous jazz operas, *Jonny spielt auf!* and *Mahagonny*. In England, William Walton and Constant Lambert wrote such jazz suites for large symphony orchestra as *Façade* and *Rio Grande*. The magic of the *Rhapsody in Blue* was irresistible. It was the greatest artistic expression of a mad and turbulent era in American life.

· 2 ·

The tumult and the shouting have not died. The *Rhapsody* is today the best-loved, the most frequently performed, and the best-known American work in the symphonic repertoire. Twenty years ago it caught on because it was a novelty, a pioneer work, a prophetic pronouncement of jazz's future. But it has survived during these years—and, one suspects, it will continue to survive for many years to come—because it is essentially much better music than we suspected when first we heard it.

Time has by no means obscured its technical shortcomings—shortcomings which, as was first believed, would doom the work to early oblivion. There are occasional schoolboyish harmonizations, the structure is often loose, the development is sometimes awkward. On the other hand, there are numerous American works with technical adroitness, a suave and polished style, elegant workmanship—works which nevertheless have long ago been forgotten. They have been forgotten because they never possessed the quality found to such a marked degree in the *Rhapsody*; that quality is *vitality*.

The vitality of the *Rhapsody* is deathless. The music remains as buoyantly fresh, as energetic, as pulsatingly dramatic today—after a hundredth hearing—as it was when first we came into contact with it. And it remains fresh because (though we hesitated to believe it) it is, at its best moments, a work of inspiration. The principal themes are striking for their originality, dash, voltaic energy; because they were fired with the spark of true genius, they still glow hot and warm us each time we listen to them. Take, for example, the very opening clarinet wail *—as marked

a touch of genius in setting forth the mood and atmosphere of the entire work as, say, the volcanic opening bars of Richard Strauss's *Don Juan*. Or the rhythmic patterns, whose ingenious subtlety gives the music its irresistible dynamism.

* Music copyright by Harms, Inc.—used by permission.

But beyond this, the music moves with a lusty pace from the opening clarinet subject to the exciting coda which brings the work to a close. It never lags. It never falls into monotony. From the first bar to the last it remains music of high tensions, alive with electric currents.

Gershwin did not, in this work, sound any one string exclusively; the *Rhapsody* has variety of mood and atmosphere. It is, of course, brilliantly witty and satiric. But it is more than that. It has its moments of intense drama; moments of introspection, as in some of the piano cadenzas; moments of tender beauty, the most unforgettable of which is the famous

slow section.* Its pages of hilarity and jovial abandon are beautifully tempered by other pages of rare grace and charm.

* Music copyright by Harms, Inc.—used by permission.

Most important of all, the *Rhapsody* is an American musical expression, so authentically conceived and projected with such American raciness and tang that we feel, when we listen to it, that a part of all of us has been caught here.

· 3 ·

Was the *Rhapsody in Blue* just a happy accident?

Many believed that it was, that in this one work Gershwin had exhausted his powers as a serious composer. Some, on the contrary, were convinced that this was but the prelude to greater things to come.

In the latter group belonged America's leading musical figure, Walter Damrosch, conductor of the New York Symphony Society. So convinced was Damrosch of Gershwin's gifts that he offered him a contract for a piano concerto to be ready the following season for performance with his orchestra.

Gershwin signed the contract eagerly. He, too, had heard people say that another work like the *Rhapsody* could not be expected from him. He even heard malicious rumors—inspired, for the most part, by envy—which insisted that the *Rhapsody* was actually not *his* work but that of Ferde Grofé, the arranger; nor did the fact that Grofé himself laughed at the rumor altogether silence it.

The only way to convince such critics was to write a larger and more ambitious work than the *Rhapsody*. A concerto—a concerto for piano and orchestra—was his new goal. If it should prove as successful as its predecessor, Gershwin knew that he would have proved to the world (and to himself) that he was a *real* composer. Then, one day after he had signed his contract, he went out to buy a textbook on musical forms in order to learn what a concerto really was!

Meanwhile Gershwin continued working for Broadway. His biographer Goldberg picturesquely described him as a "young Colossus bestriding American music, with one foot in Tin-Pan Alley, and the other in Carnegie Hall." In less than two years he produced four musical scores for successful shows, among them *Lady, Be Good* (1924), *Tip-Toes* (1925), and *The Song of the Flame* (1925). He went across to London several times, once to write a score for a production called *Primrose* (also a tremendous success), and twice to prepare some of his Broadway shows for English presentation.

He was a dynamo of energy and activity. Working on several different things at one time stimulated him, made him work all the better. In between song and stage routines, in between rehearsals and first nights, he worked patiently on the first piano concerto ever to be written in a jazz idiom. He refused to make any compromises or concessions. He was determined to write a work following the traditional concerto form, and to write as fine a work as he was capable of. He would go even further with the concerto than with the *Rhapsody:* he would orchestrate every single note himself.

With the rough draft of his music on paper, Gershwin decided to take no chances. He wanted to make certain that what he had put down on paper was what he had had in mind, to assure himself that the music *sounded* as well as it looked on paper. He therefore hired a theater for an afternoon, engaged sixty professional musicians, and asked his friend the conductor Bill Daly to rehearse the work. Now, as he listened to this orchestra, he kept revising the manuscript—cutting, editing, improving. After many hours, satisfied that the concerto had reached its final shape, he called it a day and announced that the work was ready for public performance.

The Damrosch concert took place at Carnegie Hall on December 3, 1925. The hall was packed with music lovers, jazz lovers, and curiosity seekers. As the first works on the program were being performed (a symphony by Glazunov, and a smaller work by Henri Rabaud), George nervously paced the floor of the artists' room, stopping once in a while to exercise his fingers on the piano keyboard. Ernest Hutcheson, the famous American pianist, was there with him, smiling with amusement at George's anxiety. "Don't worry, George," Hutcheson kept saying; "today you'll show them all a thing or two."

George ran his fingers through his hair. "I'm so afraid I'll make a fool of myself out there—me with my Concerto!"

Later, when Damrosch had returned from the stage, the white-haired musician whispered to George: "You have nothing to worry about, George. Not a thing. Just play the Concerto as well as it deserves, and you'll come off with flying colors."

No one has provided a more eloquent interpretation of Gershwin's artistic achievement in his concerto than Damrosch himself, who wrote as follows for the program notes:

"Various composers have been walking around jazz like a cat around a plate of hot soup, waiting for it to cool off, so that they could enjoy it without burning their tongues, hitherto accustomed only to the more tepid liquid distilled by cooks of the classical school. Lady Jazz, adorned with her intriguing rhythms, has danced her way round the world, even as far as the Eskimos of the North and the Polynesians of the South Sea Islands. But for all her travels and her sweeping popularity, she has encountered no knight who could lift her to a level that would enable her to be received as a respectable member in musical circles.

"George Gershwin seems to have accomplished this miracle. He has done it boldly, by dressing this extremely independent and up-to-date young lady in the classic garb of a concerto. Yet he has not detracted one whit from her fascinating personality. He is the prince who has taken Cinderella by the hand and openly proclaimed her a princess to the astonished world, no doubt to the fury of her envious sisters."

George played magnificently that afternoon. He always played his music with wonderful zest and spirit. His nervousness seemed now to have given him additional sparkle and brilliance. The concerto emerged from under his leaping fingers a brilliant, witty, moody, sensitive work. The audience was thrilled.

But the critics were not quite so excited. They confessed that it was a more ambitious work than the *Rhapsody*, and that, in occasional passages—the slow movement, for example—it reached greater heights of artistic expression. But they found in the music echoes of other composers—Debussy especially. And they were once again disturbed by Gershwin's shortcomings: his technical inadequacy, his formlessness, his conventionality.

One critic, however, recognized the truth that, though this work had faults, there gleamed behind them the shining light of true creative genius; listeners who were sufficiently patient with the obvious flaws to search beyond them were rewarded by music of original stamp, and often of moving beauty. This was Samuel Chotzinoff.

"His shortcomings are nothing in the face of the one thing he alone of all those writing the music of today possesses," wrote Chotzinoff (and now, more than fifteen years later, we have come to realize the full wisdom of this appraisal). "He alone actually expresses us. He is the present, with all its audacity, impertinence, its feverish delight, in its motion, its lapses into rhythmically exotic melancholy. He writes without the smallest hint of self-consciousness. . . . And here is where his genius comes in, for George Gershwin is an instinctive artist who has that talent for the right manipulation of the crude material he starts out with, that a lifelong study of counterpoint and fugue never can give to one who is not born with it."

Several years later the eminent English conductor, Albert Coates, compiled a list of the fifty best musical works of our generation. On that list, the name of only one American composer appeared—that of Gershwin; and Gershwin was represented by his Concerto.

The gifted singer, Marguerite d'Alvarez, expressed her enthusiasm for the Concerto even more forcefully. At this time the Reverend John Roach Straton of New York City was condemning jazz as

"intellectual and spiritual debauchery, utter degrada-
tion." To this charge, Marguerite d'Alvarez retorted
simply, "When I die, I want nothing better than that
Gershwin's jazz piano concerto be played over my
grave."

CHAPTER VI

"I'm a Typical Self-made American . . ."

· 1 ·

GEORGE GERSHWIN was sitting on top of the world, both figuratively and literally. Figuratively—because he was now recognized as the greatest living American composer, as well as one of the most successful. Literally—because he had taken for himself a luxurious penthouse apartment on Riverside Drive, from the terrace of which he could look down upon the winding Hudson River, and upon the heart of the metropolis wearing its many lights like a diamond brooch.

He was rich, earning often as much as a quarter of a million dollars a year from his music. He was famous. He was respected. He had won the high esteem of the greatest musicians and critics; for even those who had quibbled about the merits of the *Rhapsody* and the Concerto could not deny that he had great talent. Hardly a great musical personality came to New York without calling at Gershwin's apartment to make his acquaintance and to hear him play his music. In Tin-Pan Alley he was envied—and imitated.

This apartment, handsomely furnished in modern style, was usually filled with visitors—a strange potpourri of the great and the near-great from every walk of life. Eminent artists of the concert stage mingled with jazz-band leaders; world-famous serious composers and theorists rubbed elbows with Tin-Pan Alley musicians; moving-picture and stage stars moved among Social Registerites, and bankers and stockbrokers among Gershwin's boyhood chums and relatives from the East Side. Each of these different elements liked George and respected him, enjoyed his company, looked upon him as one of their own. In their midst, he moved with grace, spreading about him the warmth of his personality, creating a rare atmosphere of good will and affection which put even a total stranger at his ease.

He remained modest and unassuming, despite fame and fortune, more critical of himself and his music than even his severest critics. DuBose Heyward, the famous playwright and novelist, characterized him aptly when he described him as "a young man of enormous physical and emotional vitality, who possesses the faculty of seeing himself quite impersonally and realistically, and who knows exactly what he wants and where he is going. This characteristic puts him beyond modesty and conceit."

He was always considerate and fabulously generous. He supported whole branches of his family up to the end of his life. He spent several fortunes subsidizing worthy young composers and talented young musicians. Every worthy cause found him an eager contributor. Not much publicity has been given to his open hand and pocketbook, for he refused to have his generosity exploited; most of his benefactions were unknown even to his intimate friends until after his death. His door was not closed to anyone who wanted to see him—not to the sycophant, to the needy coming for a touch, to the schoolgirl wishing to express her admiration, nor even to the youngster seeking an interview for his school paper. And Gershwin was as generous with his time as with his money. The meek of the earth he welcomed as warmly as the great, for George never forgot that he himself had once lived on the East Side.

Though not a handsome man, he was attractive-looking. His eyes were soft and mobile; his face was sensitive. It was an expressive face, for he was never very astute in concealing his feelings. An aquiline nose descended sharply from an expansive brow to full lips, whose ends were gently turned in a sort of Mephistophelean smile. His dark, shining hair was brushed back. His assertive jaw, brisk walk, and vigorous handshake revealed energy and vitality. He was well built, body and muscles disciplined by exercise. One of the rooms in his new apartment was a small gymnasium where he kept fit through daily setting-up routine, boxing, punching the bag, and the like.

Not even his growing fame could tempt him to give up his native simplicity. Attitudes of grandeur were never a part of his character. He dressed unostentatiously, sometimes in tweeds, at other times in dark blue with a gray pencil stripe. Unlike many who have risen quickly from humble origins, he never lost balance or sanity. He was not extravagant, not given to display or to excesses of any kind. He never forgot his past or his background. It was charming to see that, whether he moved with leaders in the social or musical world or with some of his less fortunate relatives, he was always the same George—never flaunting his prosperity or fame, never tempted to assume airs, never given to self-publicization. His simplicity was the most striking of his many admirable traits. Sometimes in the living-room of a Park Avenue banker he would tell an amusing tale of his early East Side boyhood, when poverty and want made up his environment.

He was touchingly proud of his parents, who were always—even at his most exclusive parties—assigned places of honor. Papa Gershwin had now become a famous personality in his own right—not by virtue of any of his many business undertakings, but because of his spontaneous and unconscious wit. His innocent humor (which escaped him unawares) had made him a legend on Broadway, and anecdotes in which he figured were repeated wherever Broadway-ites gathered. There is, for instance, the story about George's hours of composing. It seems that, while George was still living with his parents, Papa Gershwin would sit on the stairs outside the room in which George was at work, holding his breath and listening raptly as the boy produced his music. If the piano played on uninterruptedly, Papa would beam with satisfaction, for then he knew that all was going well with George's inspiration. But if the piano fell silent for a few moments, Papa would go through mental torture, realizing that his George was struggling with ideas. Once, when the piano was mute for an intolerable time, Papa could contain himself no longer. Opening the door a little, he shyly thrust his plump face around it, hurriedly whistled a snatch of melody, and asked, "Does *this* help you, George?"

Some friends once tried to convince Papa Gershwin of the true greatness of the *Rhapsody in Blue*. Papa required no convincing. "Of course, it's great," he answered; "doesn't it take fifteen minutes to play?"

During the period when Einstein's theory of relativity was being talked about, George tried to impress on his father the scientist's profundity by pointing out: "Imagine, Papa, Einstein worked on his theory for more than twenty years—yet it fills only three printed pages! "Must be very small print," commented Papa tersely.

To his mother, George was particularly attached. She had a front seat at every important first performance of his music; and at its close she was traditionally the first whose congratulations he accepted. At cocktail parties or midnight gatherings in his apartment she would move with dignity and self-respect among the celebrities, and always George would exhibit her as his most prized possession. "You know," he once said wistfully, "I think that the reason why I've never gotten married is that I'm always looking for a woman like my mother—and there just *isn't* another like her!"

George's life as a successful and popular New York composer was by no means an ordered existence. His days were crowded with appointments, newspaper interviews, business conferences; and, when a show was in rehearsal, this absorbed several weeks of afternoons. He had inexhaustible energy and a nervous drive that kept him moving from one place to another, from one job to the next, without weakening his vitality. He went at a whirlwind pace, and he never seemed to tire.

When evening came, he would join some such social gathering as he himself often held in his own apartment. At these parties he would play the piano, often for hours on end, performing his earlier famous works as well as those in process of creation. He loved to play his own music for appreciative audiences, and the audiences loved to listen to him. He played his own works as no one else could, with all the zest, sparkle, enthusiasm of a man in love with his vocation.

"I've heard many pianists and composers play for informal gatherings," recalls Rouben Mamoulian, the famous stage director, "but I know of no one who did it with such genuine delight and verve. Just as a few chosen people are blessed with *joie de vivre*, so was George blessed with the joy of playing the piano. George at the piano was George happy. He would draw a lovely melody out of the keyboard like a golden thread, then he would play with it and juggle it, twist it and toss it around mischievously, weave it into unexpected intricate patterns, tie it in knots and untie it and hurl it into a cascade of everchanging rhythms and counterpoints.

"He enjoyed his playing as much as his listeners did. Nor did he ever get tired of a melody. He could play 'I've Got Rhythm' for the thousandth time, yet do it with such freshness and exuberance as if he had written it the night before. Through the whole period of *Porgy* rehearsals, whenever we got together for an evening of relaxation, George would sit down at the piano and play *Porgy and Bess* again. I remember that once during rehearsals he invited me to spend a week end with him and some friends at Long Beach. 'You must come out, Rouben, to relax and forget about *Porgy and Bess* and my music for a while,' he said. I couldn't go, but on Monday morning I asked Alexander Steinert (who had been in the party) what they had done over the week end at George's. Alex replied, 'We played *Porgy and Bess* Saturday and Sunday—all day and all night!' "

Once his mother gently reproved him for always taking the center of the stage at his parties by playing his music. "It isn't nice to be doing that all the time, George."

"But, Mother, if I don't play the piano, I just don't enjoy myself!"

Oscar Levant was characteristically acid. At a

typical Gershwin soirée, when George discussed his musical plans, talked of his ideals and aspirations, told stories about his past and his associations with musicians, dilated on his musical preferences and prejudices, and, finally, played his own music on the piano —played it endlessly, hour after hour—Oscar Levant found a momentary pause in the Gershwiniana to remark: "Tell me, George, if you had to do it all over, would you fall in love with yourself again?"

For George, composing belonged to the early hours of morning. While the rest of the city was asleep, he would work at the piano, half undressed, a cigar in his mouth. Generally, his melodies came easily; but they were worked out with the most meticulous care. Polishing them, giving them an unusual turn of melody or rhythm, cost him sweat and tears. He did not like to get down to work; it was always an effort for him. But once he had a contract, or a deadline to make, he would work like a demon. Frequently he was occupied with several tasks at once; his nervous intellect jumped from one job to another with agility. Distractions rarely affected him. He could get absorbed in his creative problems even in the midst of a houseful of guests, with several different activities going on at once. He seemed to thrive artistically when there was movement, noise, people about him. He always said that feverish New York City was the best place in the world to do work.

In the monastic seclusion of a farm in the country, George would have been unable to write down a single note, so distracted would he have been by the quiet, peace, and loneliness. He was the son of a great city, and he was at his ease only in its very heart.

He had no major vices; he never gambled (except for an infrequent game of hearts, played for low stakes), nor drank excessively. He did not enjoy idleness—or soft living. He was happiest when he had more jobs than he could handle. He did not particularly care for elaborate meals or rich foods. As a matter of fact, he was at this time—in his middle twenties—suffering from an inexplicable stomach ailment which sent him to a doctor regularly, then to a psychoanalyst, in search of an explanation and a remedy. His friends, aware that the doctor found nothing wrong with him, sometimes gently mocked him for being a hypochondriac. "You have a rich man's stomach, George," they would tell him; "there was never anything wrong with you when you were poor!" Little could they suspect then that this ailment was Nature's warning of a far more serious condition to come. . . . His sensitive stomach made him select his foods fastidiously, to choose only the simplest meals, and to eat even these sparingly.

His two self-indulgences were cigars and staying up late at night. He was fond of sports, though rather as a participant than as a spectator: he boxed a little, played a good game of basketball, enjoyed golf, tennis, and ping-pong. His hobby was painting; he had a natural bent toward this and devoted many afternoons of intensive work to his canvases. Some leading art critics have said that if Gershwin had applied himself to his painting he might easily have become a great artist. But his passion was music.

Several writers, in describing Gershwin's personality, have called him "ingenuous." This is a not altogether happy or accurate description, for it was not innocence but wisdom that gave Gershwin that unassuming self-effacement which was so often interpreted as naïveté. He was altogether incapable of putting on a false front because he had the innate gift of looking upon life, and his own career, with intelligence and balance. There was, for example, his attitude towards his own music. Even with the world's acclaim thundering at his door, he was never quite convinced of his artistic importance. True, he took pride in his achievements and his rise to success, enjoyed looking through his well-filled scrapbook, and delighted in showing people the gallery of photographs covering his study walls, inscribed with respect and admiration by notable figures in the theater, art, music, politics, and finance. But his pride never blurred the clarity of his critical perception. He knew that his technical equipment was deplorably inadequate. Time and again he talked of retiring from

Broadway to devote himself to serious study. He often felt that, for all his talent, he was little more than a creator of popular songs—charming, ingenious, often brilliantly original popular songs, perhaps, but none the less only popular songs.

When he was told that one of his songs approached greatness, he would thank his admirer quietly and would then add (it was impossible not to recognize his sincerity!) that he would gladly exchange his wealth for the talent to write songs like the "Ave Maria" or "Serenade" of Franz Schubert. He was always asking himself and others whether there was a single bar of his music that would survive him. He was all too ready to believe the less flattering criticisms which his music received. The truth is that, for all his love of talking about himself and playing his own music, Gershwin tended to underestimate himself greatly. A psychologist might easily explain his mild exhibitionism as but another reflection of his excessive modesty—an effort to convince himself that he was someone of consequence in the world of music.

· 2 ·

If Gershwin required any further proof of his increasing importance and popularity, he received it in Europe.

In the spring of 1928, when he was not quite

thirty, he took a trip abroad. What prompted the voyage was a hope that he might find the leisure to devote himself to a serious study of music. America —New York specifically—made too many demands upon him. He was a slave to his success. In its exciting, nervous atmosphere it was impossible to find the seclusion and peace necessary for study. Besides, he was constantly besieged by contracts, offers, assignments. Europe seemed to offer some measure of escape from his many social and professional duties. He went there hoping that he could, at last, find a few months in which to bury his head in textbooks.

That modesty of his made him ever painfully aware of his meager formal training. He always felt that this had been a formidable obstacle in the way of his growth as a serious composer. He had the awe for schooling which only the unschooled seem to have; it was difficult for him to realize (though many tried to tell him) that with talent and sound instincts the exceptional person can rise above an inadequate technique. Always he dreamed of giving up his work in the popular field (almost with the hopeless daydreaming of a bookkeeper who longs to abandon desk and office in order to write a great novel) so that he might fill in the yawning gaps in his musical education through some extended study.

During recent years he had tried repeatedly to acquire that musical education which he felt he had to have.   Once, while working at Remick's as a song-plugger, he plunged into the study of Bach's *Well-Tempered Clavichord*, hoping to strengthen his own compositorial technique by an analysis of Bach's methods.   Soon after this, he had become a pupil of Edward Kilenyi, who gave him his first formal training in the field of harmony.   Somewhat later, when he was already making a name for himself as a composer of popular songs, he enrolled as a student of the well-known harmony teacher, Rubin Goldmark. One day he brought Goldmark the sketches of a string quartet which he had composed some years earlier, long before he had entered Goldmark's class.   "This is very good, indeed," Goldmark told him as encouragement.   "One can see that you are already learning a great deal from this course!"

But always he was too busy and too successful to continue his studies for long.   He never seemed to find the necessary time—or the necessary patience either, for that matter.   Always he dreamed that some day in the future he might impatiently brush aside his success and turn back his contracts so as to return to the schoolroom.

Now that he was a successful composer of orchestral works, now that even the most respected critics spoke eloquently of his potentialities and promise, he felt more than ever that the time had come for him to bring his lifelong dream to realization.

But, once he stepped from the ocean liner on foreign soil, Gershwin learned that—for him—Europe meant travel, famous people to see, performances to attend. It meant the excitement of Paris, the glamour of Vienna, the historic grandeur of London, all crying to be explored. Europe even meant a new large composition which had to be written: for Gershwin was planning a symphonic poem called *An American in Paris* which the background and atmosphere of Paris was helping him to get down on paper. In such a setting, study and quiet seemed as remote and unattainable as they had been in New York.

Besides, on the infrequent occasions when he tried to acquire a teacher, he was gently discouraged. He called on Maurice Ravel, asking to become his pupil. But Ravel shook his head.

"Why do you want to become a second-rate Ravel when you are already a first-rate Gershwin?" the master asked him. "Go your own way. You don't need a teacher!"

Gershwin paid his respects also to Igor Stravinsky, who was then living in Paris. During the course of their conversation, George asked Stravinsky if he would undertake to teach him composition.

Stravinsky chuckled, and for a while he said nothing. Then, after some reflection, he asked Gershwin: "How much do you earn from your music, George?"

"Oh, about a hundred thousand dollars a year—maybe two hundred thousand."

"Well, then," retorted Stravinsky with amused irony, "in that case perhaps it is I who ought to study under you!"

No, Europe was not to offer Gershwin any answer to his educational needs, and he realized this at once. But it had other handsome compensations, for it proved an adventurous and exciting experience for the young composer, unsure of himself, and now privileged to see at first hand how widely his fame had spread.

In London, for instance, he found his musical comedy *Oh Kay* one of the triumphs of the theatrical season. Then, crossing the Channel and returning to Paris, he discovered that his *Rhapsody in Blue* was being presented as a ballet on the Champs-Elysées. What was still more gratifying, the same work was scheduled for performance at a symphony concert under the eminent conductor Rhené-Baton; the *Rhapsody* was to end the program, following a two-piano concerto by Bach.

This Rhené-Baton concert, indeed, took place on the very evening of Gershwin's arrival, so that he hardly had time to rest after his trip before making his way to the concert stage to acknowledge the excited enthusiasm of the audience—an audience which until that moment had had no hint that the American composer was in their midst. Deems Taylor was there, and he was amazed to see George walk on to the stage and bow to the applause, since he had not even known that George was in Europe.

"You can always count on George to be present when there's a bow to be taken," Taylor whispered with amusement.

Two months after the performance of the *Rhapsody*, Vladimir Golschmann conducted the Gershwin Concerto at the Paris Opera. After that concert, Gershwin enthusiasm in Paris reached almost a fever point. The newspapers devoted columns of praise to the young man from Manhattan who could write such intriguing music. Fastidious Parisian music-lovers buzzed with the excitement of discovering a major creative personality.

He was known even in Vienna. He went one evening to the celebrated Café Sacher in the company of the well-known Viennese operetta composer, Emmerich Kalman. Hardly had he stepped into the café when he heard the orchestra striking up the opening measures of the *Rhapsody in Blue*.

Lester Donahue tells an amusing incident about Gershwin in Vienna. Donahue was at the Vienna Opera attending a performance of Křenek's jazz opera, *Jonny spielt auf!* During the intermission, Donahue remarked to his friend that this music was bluff. "If a jazz opera is ever to be written," he said, rather more loudly than he meant to, "that opera will come from no one but George Gershwin."

"*Oh, yeah?*" he heard somebody behind him remark acidly.

Donahue turned sharply around and was amazed to stand face-to-face with Gershwin, who he did not know was in Europe.

"Look, George," Donahue remarked good-humoredly, "are you *always* within earshot of a compliment paid to you?"

At the Hotel Bristol in Vienna, Gershwin worked on his new symphonic poem, *An American in Paris*, which he orchestrated on his return to Paris. In this work he wanted to suggest, musically, the gaiety and effervescence of the city's spirit and the flavor of its life; he actually introduced into the score the toot of Paris taxi horns! But he wanted also to express the nostalgic yearning of an American for his own soil as he saunters along the Paris boulevards— and here he knew what he was doing, for the "American" was George Gershwin himself.

Together with his valiseful of souvenirs, George brought back from Europe the completed score of his latest large musical composition.

· 3 ·

An American in Paris was introduced at Carnegie Hall by Walter Damrosch and the New York
Philharmonic Orchestra on December 13, 1928.
The audience was loud in its approval; but, as in the
case of the Concerto, the music reviewers were divided
in their opinions. Some of them criticized the structure of the composition, regarding it as lacking in
cohesion. Others, however, commented enthusiasti-
cally. Olin Downes of the New York *Times,* for instance, found in the work a "material gain in melancholy and structure"; and Samuel Chotzinoff called
it the "best piece of modern music since Mr. Gershwin's Concerto in F."

But the piece of criticism that struck Gershwin
most forcefully, compelling him to consider his music
from a new point of view, came not from the gentle-
men of the press, nor even from a professional musician, but from that great art patron Otto H. Kahn.
At a party given in George's honor, Kahn commented
flatteringly on George's gifts and referred glowingly
to his music as an expression of "the genius of young
America." Then the philanthropist paused for a moment, reflected briefly, and wondered whether the one
thing that had so far prevented Gershwin from being
really great might not be the absence of sorrow from

his life. "The long drip of human tears, my dear George!" Kahn said softly. "They have a great and beautiful power, those human tears. They fertilize the deepest roots of art, and from them spring flowers of a loveliness and perfume that no other moisture can produce. I believe in you with full faith and admiration—in your personality, your gifts, your art, your future, your significance in the field of American music—and I wish you well with all my heart. And, just because of that, I could wish for you an experience—not too prolonged—of that driving storm and stress of the emotions, of that solitary wrestling with your soul, of that aloofness, for a while, from the actions and distractions of the everyday world, which are the most effective ingredients for the deepening and mellowing and complete development, the energizing and revealment, of an artist's inner being and spiritual powers."

Had Kahn put his finger on Gershwin's vulnerable spot—his Achilles heel—as a composer? The question continued to disturb Gershwin long after Kahn had talked to him. Undoubtedly, many of the world's greatest composers—Mozart, Beethoven, Schubert, Wagner, Tchaikovsky—had undergone emotional crises, experiences of shattering emotional impact, before they set their masterpieces down on paper; those experiences found expression in their wonderful music. And there was no doubt that, in his own music, George struck the lighter string, the more frivolous note. His best music was gay and witty. Even his most important large works were brilliantly satirical, or dynamic, or light-hearted—but poignant or tragic, never!

Could it be, mused George during these years, that his good luck was, by a curious paradox, to be his greatest misfortune? Could it be that the one thing barring him from greatness and immortality was the fact that he had never known real tragedy—that his success had come early, and that his life ever since had been a succession of uninterrupted triumphs? . . .

Yet, if his life was a parade of triumphs, it was also not without its fleeting failures; and, strange to relate, the one commercial failure that Gershwin produced was destined to become the song that today is considered his masterpiece.

The history of "The Man I Love" begins in 1924, when Gershwin wrote it for his show *Lady, Be Good*. The story goes—and it has been authenticated —that Otto Kahn was asked to provide some of the funds for the production and that he refused to do so. Shortly after this, Kahn and Gershwin happened to be aboard the same ship, returning from Europe. During the voyage George—as was almost inevitable —played some of his music for the opera patron. Kahn listened with interest to the parade of songs, then suddenly pricked up his ears at one of them and sat fascinated.

"What is that—the one you have just played?" he asked.

"It's a number called 'The Man I Love.' I wrote it for my new show. You know—*Lady, Be Good.*"

"In that case," Kahn answered, "I simply *must* finance the show."

But the song was not in the show when it reached Broadway in 1924. During the Philadelphia tryouts it had been found to lack public appeal, and it was withdrawn, and presently forgotten.

Forgotten? Not by Lady Louis Mountbatten, who chanced to hear "The Man I Love" * while she was in New York in the autumn of 1924. She was

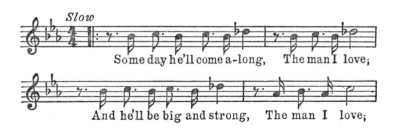

so much impressed by it that she begged George to give her an autographed copy. On her return to London early that winter, she showed the song to her

* Music copyright by Harms, Inc.—used by permission.

favorite bandleader, who forthwith featured it as one of his spot numbers. And "The Man I Love" caught on like wildfire in London. Since printed copies were not available there, one band would take it from another, learning the music by ear. And still without any printed copy in existence in England, it entered the repertoire of almost every important jazz band there.

Then, in 1927, when Edgar Selwyn was producing Gershwin's show called *Strike Up the Band!*, he asked George to incorporate "The Man I Love" in the production. It went in, was tried in out-of-town performances, and was taken out—again it had failed to make any impression on the audiences.

"The Man I Love" was destined never to become a permanent part of any Gershwin show; * and yet, by a curious irony, it grew in time to be the most famous—and the greatest—of his songs. Americans who heard it in Europe learned it there, and came back to this country singing it. Before long our own jazz bands took it up, and the oftener it was performed the more strongly its subtle and ingratiating charm appealed to the public. If Americans had not taken to "The Man I Love" at once, at least they remained faithful to it once they did take to it: of all Gershwin

* Though the buyer of phonograph records will notice that their labels usually credit the song to *Strike Up the Band!* See the Appendix, "Gershwin Records."

songs, this is the one that has achieved the most permanent popularity, and the one through which Gershwin's name is likely to become immortal in American
music, if immortality is Gershwin's fate.

CHAPTER VII

"Yankee Doodle Blues . . ."

· *1* ·

THE great Wall Street crash of 1929 was the precursor of the longest and gravest depression in American history. The seven fat years—the years of plenty—had gone forever, and 1930 ushered in the seven lean years. Hardly a phase of American life but was parched by the economic drought, hardly an American family but

135

suffered from its searing devastation. Though, by the more hopeful, the country was promised that "Prosperity is just around the corner," the depression's theme-song was "Brother, can you spare a dime?" Unemployment spread like a ravaging disease. Fortunes toppled into dust, and a favorite joke had as its butt the former banker now reduced to selling apples on the street.

But the change of Administration, three years later, to some extent revived public confidence. "The only thing we have to fear is fear itself," we were solemnly told by the new President, Franklin Delano Roosevelt, in his first inaugural address—delivered on the very day on which all the banks in the country closed in the face of an onrushing surge of panic. Soon a series of legislative dykes were being built to stem the flood. The Prohibition Amendment was repealed. The Government's responsibility to the citizen was emphasized in new social legislation; an end had come to the "rugged individualism" of the Coolidge epoch. Like so many vitamin letters, alphabets were created to cure all economic ailments: NRA, CCC, PWA, and dozens of others as time went on. The Government subsidized the arts, and out of the havoc of the depression there arose through the agency of the WPA a general movement to encourage the performance of music and drama.

It was a sober era, succeeding a drunken one. It

was a tired era which, at the end of the decade, suc-
cumbed to a new war. In some respects it was a con-
structive era, with new laws, new habits, new ideals.
"We have a rendezvous with destiny," said the President, underlining the spirit of the age. If history is a
cycle of actions and reactions, the melancholy thirties
constituted the reaction to the hysterical abandon of
the twenties. After a feverish youth, the century was
approaching maturity, and these were its "growing
pains."

· 2 ·

Yet so stable was Gershwin's fame, and his career
built on so solid a foundation, that he was not shaken
by the economic holocaust that was ravaging the country. Far from being constricted by the times, he actually expanded into new directions. As America's
leading and best-loved composer, he was now so firmly
entrenched that no force seemed capable of weakening the structure of his career.

He turned for the first time to conducting. In
1929 (a few weeks before the stock-market crash)
he made his official debut with the baton. The event
took place at the Lewisohn Stadium—home of the
summer concerts of the New York Philharmonic-
Symphony Orchestra—where, in 1927, an all-Gershwin program had been introduced. The innovation
proved so successful that the all-Gershwin program

became an annual event—and an annual event it has remained ever since. In 1927 and 1928 Gershwin himself was called on to act as piano soloist in both the *Rhapsody* and the Concerto. Then, in 1929, he was asked to take over the baton for one number, his *American in Paris*, at the concert on August 26. This was his first attempt at directing an orchestra, and it was witnessed by an audience of 20,000, establishing a new attendance record at the Stadium—just as later Gershwin concerts were always to shatter old attendance records and establish new ones. At this debut, the audience heartily approved of him as a conductor. Indeed, Gershwin took naturally to conducting, and his was a spirited and energetic performance, the men of the orchestra liking him and responding flexibly to his wishes.

That debut having gone well, Gershwin took more and more to the baton. He conducted his own orchestra on a regular radio series, during which he proved that he had a natural flair for interpreting the works of other jazz-men besides himself. In 1934 he toured the country conducting public concerts of popular music, appearing in thirty concerts within thirty days. He also undertook the direction of some of the first-night performances of his musical comedies.

Gershwin had recently associated himself for the first time with the motion-picture industry. "Talking pictures" and musical films had begun to supplant silent films, and old techniques were momentarily discarded and new ones discovered. Frantically, the industry called for help from writers, composers, actors, and offered them fabulous salaries. "California, Here I Come!" became the theme-song for Broadway's men of talent as this new Western gold rush began.

It was inevitable that Hollywood should call to Gershwin. Already the musical film had proved sensationally successful, beginning with the *Broadway Melody*. The industry was gearing itself to the production of as many musicals as possible; but musical films needed new music, and new music required the gifts of experienced composers. Hollywood was determined to purchase the best in talent. What was more natural than that it should send for the leading composer of Broadway musical comedies?

Gershwin, on going to Hollywood in 1931, was paid $100,000 to write the musical score for a Fox film called *Delicious*, starring Janet Gaynor and Charles Farrell. Gershwin liked Hollywood; and Hollywood liked Gershwin.

He composed two new major symphonic works. One of these was written during his visit to Hollywood. A sequence in *Delicious* called for a bit of atmosphere music, and, the background being New York City, Gershwin planned a short symphonic number describing the sights and sounds of a great city. He wanted to write a "rhapsody of the rivets," inspired by the rhythm of riveting. Since time lay heavy on his hands in Hollywood—the writing of several songs for the film requiring little time or effort —he decided to write a new large work for symphony orchestra, utilizing material from this episode. "Nearly everybody," he said, "comes back from California with a Western tan and a pocketful of moving-picture money. I decided to come back with these things—*and* a serious composition besides."

He rather enjoyed the idea that the Fox studios were paying him handsomely to compose his own music in his own way. The *Rhapsody in Rivets*— it was later retitled *Second Rhapsody*, the name by which it is now known—was completed in Hollywood in the summer of 1931. Gershwin rehearsed the new work in an N.B.C. studio with a specially engaged orchestra, and a private phonograph recording was made of the rehearsal. This recording, which Gershwin played and replayed in privacy, enabled him to make important revisions in the score. Early in 1932 the *Second Rhapsody*, with Gershwin as soloist, was given its world première by the Boston Symphony Orchestra under the baton of Serge Koussevitzky, and it was acclaimed by many critics as one of Gershwin's best works.

The second serious work which George wrote at

this time was the *Cuban Overture* (originally called the *Rhumba Overture*), inspired by his brief holiday in Cuba. The infectious rhythms of Cuba's dances obsessed him until he felt that he had to express them in a major work. For Gershwin, rhythmic music was a native expression, and the *Cuban Overture* was written quickly; none of his other works came so easily to him. Gershwin himself conducted the première at an all-Gershwin concert at the Lewisohn Stadium in 1932. Pitts Sanborn, New York music critic, was so delighted by the spontaneity and freshness of the music that he went so far as to say that in certain respects it was superior to Ravel's *Bolero*.

· 3 ·

Gershwin traveled in new directions even when composing music for the Broadway stage.

Since *Lady, Be Good*, in 1924, Gershwin had produced excellent musical-comedy music for shows which usually stood in the front rank of the season's smash hits: *Oh Kay* (1925), *Funny Face* (1927), *Rosalie* (1927), *Treasure Girl* (1928), and *Girl Crazy* (1930). But a Gershwin musical comedy, like all Broadway musical comedies, followed a stereotyped pattern. Invariably the book was no more than a feeble excuse to exploit set numbers, ensemble numbers, dance routines, and vaudeville skits. Neither

integration nor credibility was considered essential.
The audience was to be entertained by pleasant music,
brilliant costuming, captivating dances, and broad
humor.   It was no function of the musical comedy to
startle the audience by introducing novelty, imagination, or originality.   A Gershwin musical comedy was
exceptional only in that Gershwin music was usually
exceptional; but even here all the stage-routine formulas were religiously followed.

Then, in 1931, a new vein was opened for the
Broadway theater with a new Gershwin musicale.
George S. Kaufman and Morrie Ryskind wrote a racy
satire about politics in Washington, called *Of Thee I
Sing*, for which Gershwin was commissioned to write
the music.   It was a new type of musical-comedy book
with which Gershwin was now provided, a book which
—though it featured the usual numbers and routines
—aimed at presenting a bitingly satirical picture of
the American political scene and its backgrounds.
The time was ripe for a play like *Of Thee I Sing*.
The audiences of 1931—sad children of a nationwide depression—were eager for laughter.   Watching *Of Thee I Sing*, they could laugh to their hearts'
content at the nation's capital—which in those years
was a pretty stuffy place, full of dull politicians and
musty legislation.

But *Of Thee I Sing* was not only opportune.   It
was also fresh and novel, a sharp departure from any-

thing ever before attempted in an American musical
comedy. Its plot avoided the usual patterns, even
though it did adhere to the time-honored Broadway
theme of "boy meets girl." Wintergreen is nomi-
nated for President of the United States and, because
his party has run out of a convenient campaign program, he runs on a "love ticket." At Atlantic City
a "Miss White House" is to be selected from among
the beautiful women of America, and Wintergreen,
with Miss White House at his side, is to seek election
on this "love ticket." At the last moment, however,
he spurns the candidate chosen to be the First Lady
of the Land (Diana Devereaux) and instead takes old-
fashioned Mary Turner—because Mary can bake suc-
culent corn muffins. As he explains:

> Some girls can bake a pie
>   Made up of prunes and quinces;
> Some girls, an oyster fry;
>   Others are good at blintzes;
> Some lovely girls have done
>   Wonders with turkey stuffin's—
> But I have found the one
>   Who really can make corn muffins!

On this "love ticket" Wintergreen is elected
President by a landslide. But complications arise. In
certain parts of the country there is resentment because Diana Devereaux, the original choice for "Miss
White House," has been given a raw deal. As a

daughter of the South, she is championed by the entire bloc of Southern Senators, and—because she has French blood in her—the French Ambassador threatens to break off diplomatic relations with the United States. The feeling against President Wintergreen becomes so bitter that impeachment seems inevitable. At the critical moment, however, his wife (Mary) announces in the Senate that the President is about to become a father. Since Congress has never yet impeached an expectant father, the charges against Wintergreen are dropped—and the French are placated when Vice-President Throttlebottom takes Diana as his wife.

But it is in the detailed working out of this plot that *Of Thee I Sing* achieves brilliance. No more effective note of mockery was ever sounded on the American stage than in the treatment of Throttlebottom, the Vice-President—that "forgotten man" of American politics. He begs to be excused from running for the office because his mother might hear of it. "But," they assure him, "*no one* will *ever* hear of it!" And, after being elected, he cannot get a library card in Washington because he cannot find two references —nobody in the city knows him.

The Senate, too, gets laughed at, as when a Senator rises with dignity and reminds his fellow-members that Jenny, Paul Revere's horse, has never been granted a pension. "But," they inform him, "Jenny died in 1805"—whereupon all the other Senators rise in silent tribute to the departed Jenny.

Political rallies also are satirically criticized. During the campaign speech for Wintergreen by Senator Jones at Madison Square Garden, the audience is entertained by an exhibition wrestling match between Vidovitch and Yssevitch. Even the Supreme Court comes in for its measure of ribbing: President Wintergreen cannot have his baby until the Supreme Court has decided its sex.

For this extraordinary libretto, Gershwin wrote some of the most brilliant music of his entire career. It was as pointed in its humor as the text of the play itself, as keen-edged in its criticism of the political foibles of the day, as fleet-footed in its wit.

This was not Gershwin's first venture into musical satire. All the salient features of his musical style—his subtle use of rhythm, his light touch in melody, his original harmonic colorings—lent themselves gracefully to witty articulation. Early in his career he had written some satirical songs, such as "Mischa, Toscha, Jascha, Sascha," which poked fun at violin prodigies. And in 1927 he had written a musical-comedy score called *Strike Up the Band!*—a rousing satire against war, also by George S. Kaufman and Morrie Ryskind—in which the music reflected a persistent note of mockery. William Bolitho, the brilliant journalist, once wrote a long essay in praise of the theme-song of the show (also entitled "Strike Up the Band!") which he said was the last word in the mimicry of military marches. After hearing the music for *Strike Up the Band!*, Isaac Goldberg wrote for a stage magazine that "given a true libretto, an integrated scenario, he [Gershwin] could create for us the American equivalent of a Gilbert and Sullivan operetta."

Now, in *Of Thee I Sing*, Gershwin had a truly Gilbertian libretto, and for that libretto he wrote truly Sullivanesque music. In the opening political march,

Win-ter-green for Pres-i-dent! __

"Wintergreen for President," * in the playful "Supreme Court Judges" number (in which the staid and dignified judges are made to dance on the steps of the Capitol), popular music in America acquired an altogether new status. Others besides Goldberg now referred to Gershwin as America's Sullivan.

When the producer Sam H. Harris first discussed this show with Gershwin and the two authors, he shook his head sadly. "You know what a flop *Strike Up the Band!* was," he reminded them. "Broadway audiences just don't go in for that type of sophistication. They don't want smartness and brilliance in

* Music copyright by Harms, Inc.—used by permission.

their musical comedies. They want stock jokes, beautiful girls, and sprightly music. But if you people
want to write the show, well, I'll produce it for you—
and to hell with the expense."

But *Of Thee I Sing* was no flop! Indeed, it
proved to be one of the greatest musical-comedy successes of the year. It ran for two full seasons on
Broadway; then, following a long road tour, it was
revived for another reign on Broadway. It was the
first musical comedy to be published in book form.
Then it became the first musical comedy ever to win
the Pulitzer Prize as the best play of the year.

No wonder they were saying around Broadway
that the Gershwin touch was a magic touch. Whatever it came into contact with turned, as in the Midas
story, into pure gold. He had achieved success before
he had had an opportunity to struggle for it. And
success, from then on, clung to him tenaciously, so
that even his failures became—through some inexplicable magic—triumphs. Years before, he had
written a song called "Swanee" which seemed destined to be a failure; and overnight Al Jolson, through
the charm of his personality, made that song a coun-
trywide hit. Another apparent failure, "The Man I
Love," became a few years later the most permanently
successful of Gershwin's songs. He had written the
Rhapsody in Blue almost in spite of himself and
against his own judgment, largely as a concession to

his friend Paul Whiteman—and the *Rhapsody* earned him a million dollars. Now, finally, *Of Thee I Sing* —recognized as an uncommercial venture—proved gilt-edged security for its authors, in prestige and honor and financial profits.

George could do no wrong, they kept saying on Broadway. George was fortune's favorite, the darling of the gods.

CHAPTER VIII

"*The Real American Folk Song . . .*"

· 1 ·

EVER since his early one-act experiment in opera, seen for just one night at the *Scandals*, Gershwin had been ambitious to write an American opera—an opera whose libretto and music would arise from strictly American backgrounds and experiences. Earlier in his career he put off fulfilling his ambition until he should acquire more experience in the writing of serious music. To Jerome Kern he once said wistfully: "I wonder if I'm ready to write an opera. I have some talent—and a great deal of nerve."

But after he had become the successful composer of two rhapsodies, a piano concerto, a symphonic poem, and an overture, he felt that perhaps the time had come for the writing of his largest and greatest work. He began hunting for an appropriate libretto. For a while, he thought of writing music for a Yiddish play called *The Dybbuk* which had been translated into English and had enjoyed a successful run in New York. But an Italian composer had the exclusive opera rights to that play, and the project had to be forgone. Then he thought of using some text with the setting of a large American city (the "melting-pot" of all races and creeds) with a typical American family as principal characters. He found nothing that answered these conditions—nothing, that is, which would have lent itself to musical treatment. And he waited for the proper book to come along.

The urge to write an opera—perhaps the first *real* American opera—became more and more irresistible. He was further spurred on by the encouragement of his many friends and admirers. He had been performed at Aeolian Hall, Carnegie Hall, Symphony Hall in Boston, Lewisohn Stadium, and other American concert auditoriums. Why not at the Metropolitan Opera House? The idea exhilarated Gershwin—for it would mean the greatest artistic triumph of all.

He remembered a Theatre Guild play he had seen in New York. It was by DuBose Heyward and its title was *Porgy*. It told of the love of a crippled Negro beggar in Charleston, South Carolina, for a girl named Bess. The play had moved him—as it had moved capacity audiences for about a year—because of its American flavor, its simplicity, its picturesque background. George also recalled that at the time he saw the play he had met the author and said to him, "Some day, when I learn how, I'd like to write an opera about Porgy."

Why not an opera about Porgy? Richard Wagner had written an opera about the love of Tristan for Isolde; Debussy about that of Pelléas for Mélisande. Suddenly Gershwin realized that the love of humble Porgy for Bess was in its own way as eloquent and as touching as those of other opera heroes. Why should he not write an American love story with a Negro setting and Negro characters? It could become an American folk opera, with an American setting, rich with American musical lore. In the opera-pageant of great lovers, why should not Porgy and Bess join Tristan and Isolde, and Pelléas and Mélisande?

Once he knew what his libretto would be, Gershwin became restive, impatient to set to work upon what he knew must be his most ambitious undertaking.

There was the problem of whipping together a suitable libretto from the original play. But that could be left to DuBose Heyward himself, in collaboration with George's brother Ira, who would also write the song lyrics. Impatiently, George dropped all other work, brushed aside about a quarter of a million dollars' worth of contracts, and began to sketch the broad outlines of his opera.

The musical ideas did not come easily, for what Gershwin wanted was something richer and deeper than jazz music. He wanted his music to interpret a race, its nobility and naïveté, its heroism and cruelty, its savagery and tenderness. Such music, he felt at last, could not be plucked out of the atmosphere of New York City as the *Rhapsody* and the Concerto had been. He must familiarize himself with the local color of South Carolina, live with the folk music of the Negro until it became a part of him, come to know Negro people well and personally.

He abandoned his luxurious duplex apartment on East 72nd Street, took the train for the South, and rented a shack in the bleak setting of the waterfront near Charleston.

"Under the baking suns of July and August," DuBose Heyward recalled later, "we established ourselves on Folly Island, a small barrier island ten miles from Charleston. James Island, with its large population of primitive Gullah Negroes, lay adjacent, and furnished us with a laboratory in which to test our theories, as well as an inexhaustible source of folk material.

"The most interesting discovery to me, as we sat listening to their Spirituals, or watched a group shuffling before a cabin or a country store, was that to George it was more like a homecoming than an exploration. The quality in him which had produced the *Rhapsody in Blue*, in the most sophisticated city in America, found its counterpart in the impulse behind the music and bodily rhythms of the simple Negro peasant of the South.

"The Gullah Negro prides himself on what he calls 'shouting.' This is a complicated rhythmic pattern beaten out by feet and hands as an accompaniment to the Spirituals, and is indubitably an African survival. I shall never forget the night when, at a Negro meeting on a remote sea island, George started shouting with them—and eventually to their huge delight stole the show from their champion 'shouter.' I think that he is probably the only white man in America who could have done it. .

"Another night as we were about to enter a dilapidated cabin that had been taken as a meeting house by a group of Negro Holy Rollers, George caught my arm and held me. The sound that had arrested him was one to which, through long familiarity, I attached no special importance. But now, listening to it with him, and noticing his excitement, I began to catch its extraordinary quality. It consisted of perhaps a dozen voices raised in loud rhythmic prayer. The odd thing about it was that while each had started at a different time, upon a different theme, they formed a clearly defined rhythmic pattern, and that this, with the actual words lost, and the inevitable pounding of the rhythm, produced an effect almost terrifying in its primitive intensity. Inspired by the extraordinary effect, George wrote six simultaneous prayers producing a terrifying primitive invocation to God in the face of hurricane."

Having saturated himself with Negro music and ritual in Charleston, George could write music for his opera rich with Negroid flavors and colors. His melodies assumed the naïve patterns, and expressed the simple joys and pathos, of the Spiritual. His street cries reproduced the strange and haunting intervals intoned by vendors of fish and cakes in Catfish Row. His rhythms assumed the barbarous and savage passion of the "shouting" Gullahs. He was writing folk music of a race, and writing it with such authenticity that, in its final form, it seemed to be the work not of an American born and raised in city streets but that of several generations of Negroes who had passed these melodies from father to son.

· 2 ·

Gershwin worked for eleven months on the score of his opera, writing part of it in South Carolina and other parts in various sections of the country from upper New York to Florida. Another nine months were consumed in orchestrating it. Finally, the opera was finished. Gershwin handled the seven hundred pages of closely written music—and he felt it was good.

It had been contracted for by the Theatre Guild, which had produced the original play. Rouben Mamoulian, who had directed the original dramatic production, was once again called upon to supervise.

Mamoulian has eloquently described his first impressions of Gershwin's music to the opera as he heard George himself play it on the piano.

"It was rather amusing how we were trying to be nonchalant and poised that evening, yet we were trembling with excitement. The brothers handed me a tall highball, and put me in a comfortable leather armchair. George sat down at the piano, while Ira stood over him like a guardian angel. George's hands went up in the air about to strike the shining keys. Halfway down, he changed his mind, turned to me and said, 'Of course, Rouben, you must understand it is very difficult to play the score. As a matter of fact, it's really impossible. Can you play Wagner on the piano? Well, this is just like Wagner.' I assured George that I understood. Up went his nervous hands again, and the next second I was listening to the opening piano music of the opera.

"I found it so exciting, so full of color and so provocative in its rhythm, that after this first piano section was over, I jumped out of my armchair and interrupted George to tell him how much I liked it. Both brothers were as happy as children to hear words of praise—though Heaven knows they should have been used to them by then. When my explosion was over and they went back to the piano, they both blissfully closed their eyes before they continued with the lovely 'Summertime' song. George played with the most beatific smile on his face. He seemed to float on the waves of his own music, with the southern sun shining on him. Ira sang—he threw his head back with abandon, his eyes closed, and sang like a nightingale. In the middle of the song George couldn't bear it any longer and took over the singing from him. To describe George's face while he sang 'Summertime' is something that is beyond my capacity as a writer. *Nirvana* might be the word. So it went on. George was the orchestra and sang half the parts. Ira sang the other half. Ira was also frequently the audience.

"It was touching to see how he, while singing, would become so overwhelmed with admiration for his brother that he would look from him to me with half-open eyes and pantomime with a soft gesture of the hand, as if saying, '*He* did it. Isn't it wonderful? Isn't *he* wonderful?' George would frequently take his eyes away from the score and watch me covertly, and my reaction to the music, while pretending that he wasn't really doing it at all. It was far into the night before we finished with the opera, and sometimes I think that in a way this was the best performance of it I ever heard. We all felt exultantly happy. The next morning both George and Ira had completely lost their voices; for two days they couldn't talk, they only whispered. I shall never forget that evening—the enthusiasm of the two brothers about the music, their anxiety to do it justice, their joy at its being appreciated, and with it all their touching devotion to each other. It is one of those rare, tender memories one so cherishes in life."

Then began the round of rehearsals, with Todd Duncan and Anne Brown heading an all-Negro cast, and Alexander Smallens conducting. For several weeks, George knew all the frustrations, the heartbreak, and (gradually) the exhilaration of seeing his work emerge into life. He was gentle and softspoken, offering his criticisms quietly, rarely losing patience. When rehearsals went well, he would sit in the back of the darkened auditorium, his eyes closed as he drank in the music. But there were times when things did not go smoothly, and he would then pace the aisles nervously, the muscles of his face taut.

At last the performance was in shape; even Gershwin was satisfied. The Boston tryout, on September 30, 1935, was highly successful; at the end of the performance the audience rose to its feet to cheer the composer. Then came the New York premiere—at the Alvin Theatre on October 10.

Many in that first-night audience were puzzled by what they saw and heard. Some complained that this was not really an opera but some hybrid product combining elements of the musical comedy with those of opera. Others considered it too realistic for the make-believe world of the music-drama: who ever heard of a crap game in an opera—and a crap game treated musically through a respectable fugue?

Perhaps it was still too early for the audience to realize that they were witnessing something new—an American folk opera, treated with American realism and flavor. It had always been the fate of opera— when it attempted to strike for new directions—to be misunderstood by audiences who heard it for the first time. Eighteenth-century listeners said of Gluck's *Orfeo* that it was not an opera because the composer sought new avenues for dramatic expression. In the same manner the nineteenth century criticized Debussy, Wagner, Charpentier. And the twentieth was now complaining about Gershwin's work.

As a serious opera—so some critics said—*Porgy and Bess* had numerous dramatic and musical weaknesses: the various numbers, both solo and ensemble, were loosely assembled; there were pages that lacked artistic conviction; the recitatives were sometimes awkward. "The work," wrote Olin Downes, "does not utilize all the resources of the operatic composer or pierce very often to the depths of the simple and pathetic drama." But, in a second critical article about the work, Mr. Downes realized that "this is an opera with real melodies in it. . . . In his own way and according to his own lights, Mr. Gershwin has taken a substantial step, and advanced the cause of native opera."

But if, at its opening performance, *Porgy and Bess* had not received the acclaim it deserved, it was not to be permanently denied its due measure of fame. It was revived in 1938 in Los Angeles and San Francisco with the original New York cast, and was acclaimed by both cities. In 1937 the David Bispham Silver Medal was awarded to *Porgy and Bess* as an outstanding native achievement in the field of opera. Early in 1942 it was revived in New York and it proved sensationally successful, one of the most substantial hits of the dramatic season, enjoying the longest run ever had by a "revival." The Music Critics' Circle of New York singled it out as the most important musical "revival" of the year.

· 3 ·

Porgy and Bess is an opera about America, with the simplicity, beauty, tender humor, wistfulness, and pathos of great folk art. Gershwin himself called it, appropriately, a folk opera. "I have been asked why it is so called," he wrote. "The explanation is a simple one. *Porgy and Bess* is a folk tale. Its people naturally would sing folk music. When I first began work on the music I decided against the use of original folk material because I wanted the music to be all of one piece. Therefore I wrote my own Spirituals and folk songs. But they are still folk music—and therefore, being operatic in form, *Porgy and Bess* becomes a folk opera."

It is now recognized that it is one of the most successful examples of native American opera. For two centuries, American composers have written operas; but rarely have they written *American* operas. The texts they used were frequently remote from American experiences. Even when composers wrote operas about American subjects—like Walter Damrosch in *The Scarlet Letter*, or Victor Herbert in *Natoma*, or Charles Wakefield Cadman in *Shanewis* —the music was but a pale imitation of European models. But Gershwin's opera could have been written only by an American; and its music has roots deeply embedded in American soil.

Some far-sighted musicians, even from the first, realized the full importance of Gershwin's opera. "The musical influence of George Gershwin's *Porgy and Bess*," wrote J. Rosamund Johnson, "will live through the ages and the transitions of musical vogues as a fountain of inspiration to writers. Some may differ at great length with his unusual style; nevertheless, the example and magnitude of this young man's musical exposition and development of folklore, emanating from street cries, blues, and plantation songs of the Negro, will prove itself a beacon of light to those who are brave enough to stray from the 'web-born' standards of the great masters of Europe."

Porgy and Bess may not be all of one piece; there are great pages, and there are dull ones. There may be lapses in the inspiration—some incomplete realizations of the drama, some awkward constructions, some trite expressions. But in the face of its freshness and originality these faults, and others like them, appear negligible. As Virgil Thomson commented: "Gershwin may not know what an opera is; and yet *Porgy and Bess* is an opera, and it has power and vigor. Hence it is a more important event in American artistic life than anything American the Metropolitan Opera House has ever done." *Porgy and Bess* is a great folk opera. It is our *Boris Godunov*, our *Bartered Bride*. . . .

That genial patron of the arts in general and of

opera in particular, Otto H. Kahn, did not live long enough to hear *Porgy and Bess;* he died a year before its first performance.   Had he lived, he would have been the first to admit that with that work George had entered the halls of greatness.   It is a more mellow artist who composed *Porgy and Bess* than the one who wrote either the *Rhapsody in Blue* or the Concerto. George had outgrown the expression of a nervous, high-pitched era.   The music of *Porgy* is not the interpretation of any one limited period.   In his earlier works, Gershwin had been the slave of jazz: it dominated his thoughts, his feelings.   In *Porgy and Bess*, Gershwin was its master, using it with sparing economy to serve his artistic purpose.

That there were eloquent melodies in *Porgy and Bess* was to be expected from Gershwin—and songs like "Summertime" and "I Got Plenty o' Nuttin' " are in his best lyric vein.   That there was fleet wit was also to be expected.   But there were these things, and some things more—moments as in the Wake Scene or at the close of the opera when an artist speaks with an intensity of speech and deeply moving emotion.

Yes, Otto H. Kahn would have been the first to acknowledge that in *Porgy and Bess* Gershwin had produced a work of art.   And Gershwin had succeeded in producing it without experiencing personal tragedy. . . .

CHAPTER IX

"My Man's Gone Now . . ."

· 1 ·

AFTER *Porgy and Bess*, Gershwin spent most of his time in Hollywood, working for the movies. He had returned to the Coast in 1936 to prepare a score for the Fred-Astaire–Ginger-Rogers musical, *Shall We Dance?* It was his first contact with the movies since 1931. Once again, he liked working for the films. He produced songs in his best and most engaging vein: gay, wistful, poignant Gershwin tunes like "Shall We Dance?" and "Let's Call the Whole Thing Off," nimbly projected on the screen by the tapping toes of Astaire and Rogers. In 1937 he wrote music for another Fred Astaire film, *A Damsel in Distress*. Then he was contracted by Samuel Goldwyn to write the score for a lavish screen musical, *The Goldwyn Follies*.

During the summer of 1937, while working on the music for the *Follies* at the Goldwyn studios, Gershwin suddenly and mysteriously collapsed one morning. His illness was diagnosed as a mild nervous breakdown. Walter Winchell announced George's physical collapse over the radio, and an entire country held its breath. Apprehension was assuaged when Mother Gershwin announced to the newspapers that Gershwin's sickness was really nothing much: He had worked too hard; he was tired; he needed quiet and rest. As a matter of fact, George emerged from his illness magically. After a few days of seclusion, he had recovered so completely that his physicians permitted him to return to work.

Beyond that strange, sudden collapse, Gershwin gave no indication of being a sick man. Well, he *had* been suffering from some headaches; and there was still that old stomach ailment of his. But neither of these seemed an important symptom. For the most part he was cheerful, energetic, and full of his usual gusto. He played tennis with verve, a forceful and accurate game which taxed the stamina of his opponents. To see him run briskly across the courts and powerfully return his opponent's drive was to be convinced (as so many of his friends were convinced) that there could not possibly be anything wrong with his health. He was a frequent guest at the homes of Hollywood's movie stars, and now, as before, he was an indefatigable entertainer at the piano.

Above all this, he was talking sanguinely about his future. There were so many new and ambitious works that he longed to write! *Porgy and Bess* had finally convinced him that he was capable of writing important music. What he had already done, George now felt, had merely been his apprentice works. Now he had found his stride. He was eager to move briskly.

To prepare himself more fully for the important assignments he was revolving in his mind, he had already undertaken the study of theory with Joseph Schillinger, and it was the most thorough technical training he had ever had—training that brought to him all the modern techniques of composition. He spent diligent hours working over his laborious exercises, determined once and for all to be a master of his craft.

The future, therefore, looked even more impressive than his brilliant past.

He had only just begun to live, to work, to create. . . .

· 2 ·

On Saturday morning, July 10, 1937, while still at his home, George collapsed a second time. In a coma, he was rushed to the Cedars of Lebanon Hospital in Hollywood. There he disclosed some startling symptoms. The X-Rays revealed that a tumor was growing on his brain, and a group of surgeons decided that an operation was imperative; but they hoped to postpone it long enough to bring the famous surgeon, Dr. Walter E. Danby, from the East by plane.

Hurried telephone calls to the East brought word that Dr. Danby was cruising on a yacht on Chesapeake Bay with the Governor of Maryland. George's life was hanging by a hair. Frantically his physicians appealed to the Coast Guard to search thoroughly for Dr. Danby; he was eventually found, and taken by plane to Newark, N. J. Here he immediately established contact by telephone with the Lebanon Hospital, listened carefully to the physicians' description of the case, and gave his judgment: "It is too late for me to get to California and operate—but Gershwin *must* be operated on at once, and the sooner the better!"

The operation was performed by Dr. Carl Rand, who skillfully removed a cystic tumor from the right temporal lobe of the brain. It was delicate surgery; but it had come too late. Had the tumor been detected a few months earlier—perhaps even a few weeks—the operation might well have been successful. As it was, the odds were preponderantly against Dr. Rand when he put scalpel to Gershwin's brain; and he lost.

Gershwin never returned to consciousness. At 10:35 on the following morning—July 11—he stopped breathing; his brother Ira being at his bedside to the last. George died without learning that he had been given Italy's highest award to a foreign composer —an honorary membership in the St. Cecilia Academy of Music in Rome.

From one end of the country to the other came expressions of grief. Over a radio network there were special Gershwin Memorial Programs in which many leading Broadway and Hollywood stars participated, including Paul Whiteman, Fred Astaire, Al Jolson, Ethel Merman, and Ferde Grofé. In New York, a few weeks later, a Gershwin Memorial Concert at the Lewisohn Stadium attracted the largest audience ever to enter the Stadium.

"Like a rare flower which blossoms forth once in a while, Gershwin represents a singularly original and rare phenomenon," said the Boston conductor,

Serge Koussevitzky. "Like a flower, his life was short-lived; but the blossom of his soul has, is, and will be an inspiration to many a renowned composer of our day and of days to come. The voice of his music spread far beyond his country; it is heard overseas. To understand the nature of his gift and his mission is to realize that Gershwin composed as a bird sings—because it is natural, it is inborn, it is a part of its being. . . . His richly endowed nature absorbed and crystallized the essence of American lore and poured it out into melody and rhythm with all the spontaneity, originality, and dynamic strength which were his own.

"Unassuming, never thinking of himself as an 'immortal,' George Gershwin was destined to influence contemporary and modern music, and to leave his footprints on the Sands of Time."

Ferde Grofé said: "I may never again meet the like of George Gershwin, a rare and refined spirit, an innovator in American music, and one who has left upon it the lasting imprint of new ideas voiced with bold originality."

Paul Whiteman lamented: "George Gershwin is gone, but his music is his enduring monument."

Olin Downes wrote as an obituary epitaph: "He will have a secure place in the American tonal art."

And from the singer, Eva Gauthier—the same Eva Gauthier who had been first to bring Gershwin's music into a concert auditorium—came the following tribute: "George Gershwin will live as long as music lives. . . . He will never be forgotten, and his place will never be filled."

· 3 ·

George Gershwin's body was sent back to New York. Funeral services were held on Thursday afternoon, July 15, at the Temple Emanu-El. More than three thousand of Gershwin's admirers—screen and stage stars, bankers, politicians, great musicians, the ordinary man of the street—crowded the Temple. Outside stood another thousand admirers who, unable to gain admission into the Temple, were none the less eager to pay their last respects to their beloved composer. It was drizzling and raw, but not many of those who stood patiently outside the Temple were aware of the discomfort. Strange! As if the elements mourned particularly the passing of its musical sons, it had rained when Mozart, when Beethoven, and when Schubert were buried. And now it was raining for the burial of George Gershwin!

Inside the Temple, there was music: a Bach air played on the organ, Schumann's *Träumerei* on the cello, the slow movement from one of Beethoven's last quartets played by strings, and finally—on the organ —the andante section of the *Rhapsody in Blue*.

"He was America's folk-musician," said Rabbi Stephen S. Wise in his eulogy, "drawing his nurture from the breast of American folk-life and all its ways. He echoed American plaints; he gave lilt in his songs to the songs of American folk."

The honorary pallbearers—who included Mayor La Guardia, ex-Mayor James J. Walker, George M. Cohan, Walter Damrosch, and Edwin Franko Goldman—carried the flower-covered coffin out of the Temple. The crowds outside, wet with the rain and sick at heart with grief, drew closer for a last fleeting contact with the man they loved. The procession to the cemetery started, holding up traffic because so many, in spite of the chill and the dampness, insisted upon following George to his last home.

*   *   *

They say that on that night a strange pall hung over Broadway—a gloom that seemed to settle over the Gay White Way like a heavy cloud, above the streets around Times Square, in night clubs, in the theaters. Some frequenters of this part of New York City who were not aware that Gershwin had just been buried noticed this phenomenon without understanding it. But thousands of other New Yorkers, who knew only too well what had happened, realized that Broadway had lost her favorite son and she was mourning her loss as keenly as were the millions throughout the country who loved George Gershwin's music.

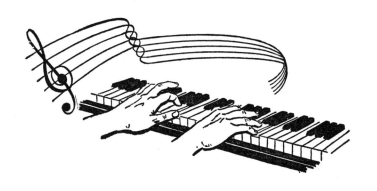

EPILOGUE

"Of Thee I Sing . . ."

· 1 ·

TWENTY years ago, several far-sighted and courageous musicians—among them Beryl Rubinstein, Carl Van Vechten, and Eva Gauthier—called George Gershwin a "great" composer. At this daring appraisal, musical circles shuddered. Twenty years ago, Gershwin had not yet written his *Rhapsody in Blue;* all he had to his credit was a series of popular song successes and the scores for several Broadway musical-comedy shows. And who had ever heard of a writer of popular songs being called a "great" composer?

Today, few will deny that Gershwin was great, one of the greatest musicians America has produced. Twenty years is a short time for the world to revise its judgment about a composer. Bach had to wait more than a hundred years for the recognition he deserved, and Schubert more than fifty. Why has the world already come to accept Gershwin so unhesitatingly as a composer of major importance?

Greatness in music may mean any of a number of things. It may mean that a composer has originality, that he has written music which is so much an expression of his personality, background, and experiences that had he never written his music we would have lost something vital and priceless. It may mean that a composer has opened up new horizons for musical expression, thereby influencing musicians around him. It may mean that a composer has achieved such universality of speech that he is loved everywhere by different classes of people.

Choose whichever definition you wish, and George Gershwin fits. He composed music of extraordinary beauty; the fact that so much of his music was written for the masses does not make it less beautiful. On all his music his personality is stamped recognizably: his way of shaping a melody, his use of rhythmic phrase. In his music are revealed his backgrounds and experiences as the son of a great, throbbing city. It is his own music, and—because he was of our times and of our setting—it is our music as well.

Who has not responded to the wonderful Gershwin songs—to the best of them at any rate—with their vein of tenderness, their irrepressible wit, their inexhaustible melodic invention, their ingenuity of rhythm and wealth of color? Who has not felt the throb of excitement, the thrill of discovering a new world, on first hearing the *Rhapsody in Blue*, the Concerto, or some of the songs from his opera, *Porgy and Bess?*

Beyond this, Gershwin has influenced the direction of modern music more than any other single composer of our time, with the possible exception of Stravinsky. When Gershwin came on the musical scene, jazz was in disrepute as a musical idiom. It was he who proved that jazz was a speech worthy of the respect of every serious musician who wished to express his times in music. Throughout the world, great composers were encouraged by his successful experiment to write large works in jazz. Following under his banner, Ravel wrote the "blues" sonata for violin and piano, and Křenek and Weill their jazz-operas, *Jonny spielt auf!* and *Mahagonny*.

There is least question of Gershwin's capacity to

appeal to audiences everywhere, to people of every class and country. He was in our own day what Johann Strauss (the second) was in his: the composer of tunes that circled the globe. The writer of this biography was again and again given evidence of Gershwin's enormous popularity throughout Europe. He recalls a visit to a Viennese outdoor café. It was such a Vienna café as was typical in the period before the First World War. Japanese lanterns shed their lights, filtered through a variety of colors. The audience was a cross-section of Viennese life: officers in their smart gray uniforms; clerks with their sweethearts; stout shopkeepers with their wives and children; university students with their university ribbons on their caps. The entertainers included a woman accordion player, a red-faced comedian, and a two-piano team. At last came the moment for the two-piano music, and the limelight was turned on the players. They played the *Rhapsody in Blue*. The injection of a raucous twentieth-century voice into an atmosphere of old Vienna seemed incongruous—but not to Viennese themselves. It was amazing to note how the audience—Viennese café audiences are notoriously noisy during a performance—suddenly became tense. All conversation had stopped, as if on a prearranged signal. Some even left off eating, so as not to disturb the music with the clatter of silverware on dishes. The waiters made no effort at serving their guests. Everyone was listening fascinated until the final note.

The writer recalls, again, a climb up the Hungerberg at Innsbruck, Austria. Below him stretched an Old World city nestling at the foot of a mountain. The place seemed far remote from twentieth-century New York, a world apart. Suddenly—as the writer was relaxing with a cup of coffee with whipped cream—the Old World seemed to vanish from his consciousness, and in its place arose the modern city of smoke and steel. A loudspeaker was pouring out the nervous accents of *Lady, Be Good*.

Just as clearly remembered are the numerous times when the writer heard Gershwin melodies in London and Paris theaters, night clubs, and dance halls, and saw how the French and the English, particularly the younger set, loved these melodies. Towards their own popular music, London and Paris audiences were usually tepid. But whenever a Gershwin tune was played they tendered unforgettable demonstrations of appreciation.

The *Rhapsody in Blue* was used in ballets in Paris and London, and was featured by numerous European symphony orchestras. In July 1931, *An American in Paris* was performed in London (and with striking success) at the ninth annual festival of the International Society for Contemporary Music. And—as has been mentioned—Italy bestowed on

Gershwin, just before his death, the highest honor it could award to a foreign composer, electing him an honorary member of the St. Cecilia Academy of Music in Rome.

Even in Nazi Germany, where Gershwin's music is officially tabu because he was not an Aryan, he is admired—surreptitiously, of course. The Countess Waldeck, in her book *Athene Palace*, quotes a high Nazi official as saying: "Do you know there is not one of us who has not a Gershwin record in the bottom of a drawer which he plays sometimes late at night?"

To Americans, of course, Gershwin's music has a particularly personal meaning. He saw America grow and develop into a great industrial country, a world power, and he was an element in that growth. No other composer spoke for our country during our times so unforgettably as he. Later generations will come to know us through his music just as today we know old Vienna through Schubert and Johann Strauss. America's nervousness, energy, youth, and strength are all revealed in his infectious rhythms, its color and background reflected in his harmonies. It is music about an age of steel and speed; it is music that gives voice to a great metropolis. It is as thoroughly American in every pore and tissue as cocktails, tabloids, night clubs, and rodeos.

· 2 ·

His was a typically American career, originating
in comparative poverty in the slums and culminating
in wealth and worldwide fame. It was the career of
a self-made man. He never had the musical education necessary for pretentious composition. He knew
his inadequacies, and they frequently tormented him.
But he did not let them stifle the music within him.
Some technique he acquired through spasmodic study;
some technique he never really mastered. But because
he had the will and the talent he rose above his shortcomings and wrote important music.

He was a composer of popular songs—a very
successful one—before he turned to the composition
of serious music. The fact that no other popular-song
composer had ever before been graduated from Tin-
Pan Alley to Carnegie Hall did not prevent him from
trying to make the grade. Almost from the moment
he began composing he seemed to know that he had
a mission to perform. He permitted neither an easy
success nor a soft life to deflect him from that mission.

Images of and about Gershwin inevitably leap
to the mind of the present writer, who knew him over
a period of many years. My memory, for example,
reaches back to the year of 1919 when I spent a brief
holiday in a summer resort in the Catskill Mountains.

I was then not much older than many of you who are now reading this book. One afternoon, one of the guests of the hotel was aimlessly improvising on the piano as I passed by. He played a catchy tune, and I stopped to listen. "Do you like it?" he asked me. I said I did. "It's by a young composer about whom nobody knows anything—yet. But remember the name. He'll become one of our greatest composers."

The name was George Gershwin. It was the first time I had ever heard it, or any of his music. But I never had the chance to forget either one, for that same year—a few months after the episode at the hotel—a song called "Swanee" was skyrocketed to nationwide fame by Al Jolson and established Gershwin's reputation.

I recall, too, a rather dull afternoon in 1924 when I went to a vaudeville show at the Palace Theatre in New York. Some "blues" singer was moaning a group of numbers which so far had done nothing to rescue the program from tedium, and probably I should long ago have forgotten both the day and the show but for one thing. Suddenly, the "blues" singer started a melody that made my heart skip a beat. It had such loveliness, such unusual structure and feeling, that I listened fascinated. Later I learned that the song was "Somebody Loves Me." That afternoon remains memorable because it marked my first realization that Gershwin had genius.

Fleeting images come and go; there was, for example, the first time I met Gershwin. I had gone to interview him. He met me with a warm and engaging manner, his eyes softly expressive, and his whole bearing one of gentle modesty. He showed a certain shyness as he talked about his career; but when he discussed his aspirations—even then it was his ambition to do something fine and important for American music through the use of the popular idiom—his eyes glowed hotly. It was impossible not to be attracted to him. He was unpretentious, sincere, and frank. I told him that I felt that he was much more than merely a composer of popular songs—not precisely an original thought, even at that time, for already several far-sighted musicians had said the same thing. "I hope you are right," he answered quietly, "for that is the one real aim of my life."

Other images of Gershwin haunt the memory. I shall select only the more vivid ones. I see him now as I saw him one afternoon in the artists' room at Carnegie Hall. It was just before the performance of the Concerto. He was pacing the room nervously. On his face was an expression which seemed to ask, "What in the world am I doing *here*, anyway?"

Again, I see him as I saw him during a rehearsal of one of his shows, slouched in a seat at the rear of the darkened theater as Bill Daly was taking the music through its paces. "Do you think the music is up to par?" he asked me nervously—once more impressing me with his extraordinary modesty.

Or I see him now as I saw him one afternoon at his apartment on Riverside Drive. I told him honestly—because I knew he demanded honesty—that I felt his *American in Paris* was inferior to his two other large works. He was not offended at all; he just listened to my opinion, and then tried to convince me that I was wrong. He played snatches of the music on the piano, pointing out the salient passages. He put the records of the work on his phonograph and singled out various moments for my scrutiny. At last he stopped one of the records in the very middle of a bar and brusquely shut off the phonograph. "You know," he said, "I'm inclined to think you're right after all!"

And I see him now as I saw him late one night after a performance of *Porgy and Bess*. I had not met him for some time. He greeted me warmly, and with his usual generosity told me how much he liked some of the things I had written. I told him how highly I thought of *Porgy*. It was his maturest work; more than that, it was one of the most impressive achievements by an American composer. "Now, George," I remember saying, "you are *really* beginning to compose."

"I think so, too," George answered with a soft laugh.

How was I to know that with *Porgy and Bess*
Gershwin had really finished?

· *3* ·

George Gershwin was fabulously honored in his
own day.   No other American composer has ever attained a like amount of adulation or material prosperity.   Success came to him early, and it remained faithful to him until his dying day.   The masses adored
his music.   The musical great of the world paid tribute to his genius.

The fame of the average composer of popular
songs dies with him.   Not so with Gershwin.   His
stature has grown rather than diminished since his
death.   If in his own day his songs were resounding
hits, by this time they have become minor classics.   In
a field where the mortality rate is high (there is nothing quite so dead as last year's song hit), Gershwin's
melodies have almost magically retained their freshness and appeal.   Today it is hardly possible to listen
to an evening of radio music without hearing at least
one of his songs, and they all sound as fresh as if they
had just been written—though actually some were
composed many years ago.

In the field of serious American music, Gershwin occupies a place of his own.   Nobody denies that
he had faults as a composer.   But faults have not kept

masters like Schumann, Tchaikovsky, or Richard Strauss from immortality. Schumann's instrumentation was frequently defective, and yet his symphonies have survived as some of the most delightful examples of nineteenth-century Romanticism. Tchaikovsky was often oversentimental, and Strauss often overdressed his orchestrations and harmonizations. Yet each of these two composers has written inspired music that lives. What is true of Schumann, Tchaikovsky, and Strauss is true also of Gershwin. Again and again he proved the inadequacy of his musical training. His musical structure was sometimes clumsy. His ideas were not always developed with imagination and richness. He often resorted to disturbing little clichés when his inventiveness gave out. But—even while recognizing these faults and lamenting them— one must still confess that they pale before his strength as a composer.

As has been said above, when the *Rhapsody in Blue* was first performed, even the many who profoundly admired it feared that at best it was only a novelty, to fall ultimately under the contempt that familiarity breeds. Yet—as this book is being published—the *Rhapsody* is about to celebrate its twentieth birthday, and it is today probably the most frequently performed serious American work in the symphonic repertoire—certainly the best known. It has survived because it has vitality, freshness of approach,

and the touch of true genius. The other large works
—*An American in Paris*, the *Second Rhapsody*, the
Concerto, the *Cuban Overture*—have also, in varying
degrees, survived their composer and retained their
appeal. And *Porgy and Bess*, when it was revived on
Broadway in 1942, surpassed the success it had enjoyed when first produced—and it was then the leading theatrical hit of the entire season. For, by 1942,
Americans everywhere had come to know many of its
melodies, and to love them as deeply as Italians love
the arias from their operas. Subsequently, principal
melodies from *Porgy* were incorporated by Robert
Russell Bennett in an orchestral suite, which was performed by the Pittsburgh Symphony under Fritz
Reiner.

One need go no further than to consider the
enormous crowds which each year attend the Gershwin Memorial concerts, taxing the capacity of hall or
stadium, to realize that since his death Gershwin is as
much loved and appreciated as he was during his life.
Obviously, he has won for himself a permanent place
in American music. It is because Hollywood realized
that Gershwin belongs with the great Americans of
all time that it decided to dedicate to him a screen
biography (in preparation as this is being published).

Once a quip used to circulate on Broadway which
mocked at George's weakness for playing his own
tunes wherever and whenever there was a group near

that cared to listen to him. "How long will Gersh-win's music live?" "As long as Gershwin is here to play it!" Well, Gershwin is no longer here. But his music still lives, is still played, still loved. Will it be alive tomorrow? Prophecy would be silly. Isn't it enough to reflect that while George Gershwin was alive he meant so much to so many people throughout the world, and that now—though dead—he is still with us, a part of us, speaking for us and our American scene through his imperishably vital music?

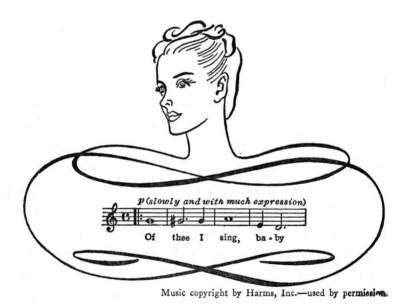

p (slowly and with much expression)

Of   thee   I   sing,   ba - by

BIBLIOGRAPHY

BOOKS

ARMITAGE, MERLE (editor): *George Gershwin.* New York, Longmans, Green & Co., 1938.

EWEN, DAVID: *Twentieth Century Composers.* New York, Thomas Y. Crowell Co., 1937.

EWEN, DAVID (editor): *The Book of Modern Composers.* New York, Alfred A. Knopf, Inc., 1942.

GOLDBERG, ISAAC: *George Gershwin.* New York, Simon & Schuster, 1931.

HOWARD, JOHN TASKER: *Our Contemporary Composers.* New York, Thomas Y. Crowell Co., 1941.

LEVANT, OSCAR: *A Smattering of Ignorance.* New York, Doubleday, Doran & Co., 1940.

ARTICLES

"American in Memoriam" by John O'Hara, in *Newsweek,* July 15, 1940.

"Gershwin" by R. Pollak, in *American Magazine of Art,* September 1937.

"George, the Ingenuous" by Alexander Woollcott, in *Cosmopolitan,* November 1933.

MUSICAL COMEDIES, REVUES, AND FILMS
FOR WHICH GERSHWIN WROTE MUSIC

A—MUSICAL COMEDIES AND REVUES FOR WHICH GERSHWIN WROTE ALL THE MUSIC

Funny Face, 1927
Girl Crazy, 1930
Half-Past Eight, 1918
Lady, Be Good, 1924
La La Lucille, 1919
Let 'Em Eat Cake, 1933
(The) Midnight Whirl, 1920
Of Thee I Sing, 1931
Oh Kay, 1925
Our Nell, 1923
Pardon My English, 1932
Primrose (London), 1924

Rainbow Revue, 1922
Rosalie, 1927
Scandals of 1920, 1921, 1922, 1923, and *1924*
Show Girl, 1929
(The) Song of the Flame, 1925
Stop Flirting (London), 1924
Strike Up the Band! 1927
Sweet Little Devil, 1924
Tell Me More, 1925
Tip-Toes, 1925
Treasure Girl, 1928

B—MUSICAL COMEDIES AND REVUES TO WHICH GERSHWIN CONTRIBUTED SONGS

Americana, 1924
Broadway Brevities, 1919
Blue Eyes, 1920
(A) Dangerous Maid, 1921
Dere Mable, 1919
Ed Wynn's Carnival, 1920
For Goodness' Sake, 1922
(The) French Doll, 1922
Good Morning, Judge, 1920

Hitchy-Koo, 1918
Ladies First, 1918
(The) Lady in Red, 1920
Little Miss Bluebeard, 1923
Look Who's Here, 1918
(The) Nifties, 1922
(The) Passing Show of 1916
(The) Perfect Fool, 1920
Sinbad, 1920

C—FILMS FOR WHICH GERSHWIN WROTE THE MUSIC

(A) Damsel in Distress, 1937
Delicious, 1931

Goldwyn Follies, 1937
Shall We Dance? 1937

GERSHWIN RECORDINGS

NOTE: All the recordings listed below are of the long-playing variety (33 1/3 rpm).

CONCERT WORKS

An American in Paris

Capitol P-303. Paul Whiteman and his Orchestra.
Columbia ML-4455. André Kostelanetz and his Orchestra.
Columbia ML-4026. New York Philharmonic Symphony under Rodzinski.
Decca L-8519. Kingsway Symphony under Camarata.
Mercury 20037. Hollywood Symphony under Newman.
Victor LPT-29. RCA Victor Symphony under Shilkret.
Victor LM-1031. RCA Victor Symphony under Bernstein.
Victor LM-9020. NBC Symphony under Toscanini.
Vox 3130. Pro Musica Orchestra under Dixon.

See also COLLECTIONS.

Concerto in F

Capitol P-8219. Pennario and Pittsburgh Symphony under Steinberg.

Columbia ML-4025. Oscar Levant and the New York Philharmonic Symphony under Kostelanetz.

Remington 199-184. Templeton and Cincinnati Symphony under Johnson.

See also COLLECTIONS.

Cuban Overture

Columbia ML-4481. André Kostelanetz and his Orchestra.

Decca 8024. Paul Whiteman and his Orchestra.

See also COLLECTIONS.

Preludes (for piano)

Columbia ML-2073. Levant.

See also COLLECTIONS.

Porgy and Bess

Complete performance: Columbia SL-162. Lawrence Winters, Camilla Williams, Inez Matthews, Avon Long, the J. Rosamond Johnson Chorus, Orchestra, under Engel.

Excerpts. Vol. 1: Decca L-7006. Original Porgy and Bess company including Todd Duncan, Anne Brown, Edward Matthews, etc., under Smallens.

Contents: Summertime; I Got Plenty o' Nuttin'; My Man's Gone Now; Buzzard Song; Bess, You Is My Woman Now; It Ain't Necessarily So; Requiem; Porgy's Lament; Finale.

Excerpts. Vol. 2: Decca L-8024. Same cast as above.

Contents: A Woman Is a Sometime Thing; It Takes a Long Pull to Get There; What You Want wid Bess?; Strawberry

Woman's Call; Crab Man's Call; I Loves You, Porgy; There's a Boat That's Leavin' Soon for New York.

Excerpts: Victor LM-1124. Risë Stevens, Robert Merrill, the Robert Shaw Chorale and the RCA Victor Symphony under Bennett.

Contents: Summertime; A Woman Is a Sometime Thing; Gone, Gone, Gone; My Man's Gone Now; I Got Plenty o' Nuttin'; Bess, You Is My Woman Now; It Ain't Necessarily So; Where Is My Bess?

See also COLLECTIONS.

Porgy and Bess: A Symphonic Picture (orchestrated by Robert Russell Bennett)

Bluebird LBC-1059. Indianapolis Symphony under Sevitzky.
Columbia ML-2019. Pittsburgh Symphony under Reiner.
Columbia 4ML-4904. New York Philharmonic Symphony under Kostelanetz.
Decca L-7002. Los Angeles Philharmonic under Wallenstein.
Decca 4051. Los Angeles Philharmonic under Green.
Mercury 50016. Minneapolis Symphony under Dorati.
Victor LM-1879. Boston Pops Orchestra under Fiedler.

Rhapsody in Blue

Bluebird LBC-1045. Janis and orchestra under Winterhalter.
Capitol P-303. Pennario and Paul Whiteman Orchestra.
Columbia 4ML-4455. Templeton and Kostelanetz Orchestra.
Columbia 4ML-4026. Levant and Philadelphia Orchestra under Ormandy.
Coral 56053. Wild and Paul Whiteman Orchestra.
Decca L-8024. Bargy and Paul Whiteman Orchestra.
Decca L-8519. Sandford and Kingsway Symphony under Camarata.

Victor LPT-29. Gershwin and Paul Whiteman Orchestra.
Vox 3130. Rivkin and Pro Musica Orchestra under Dixon.

See also COLLECTIONS.

Rhapsody in Blue (transcribed for two pianos)

Victor LM-23. José and Amparo Iturbi.

Second Rhapsody

Columbia ML-2073. Levant and Morton Gould Orchestra.
Decca L-8024. Bargy and Paul Whiteman Orchestra.

See also COLLECTIONS.

Variations on I Got Rhythm

Columbia ML-2073. Levant and Morton Gould Orchestra.

COLLECTIONS

Ella Sings Gershwin

Decca DL-5300. Ella Fitzgerald.

Contents: Someone to Watch Over Me; My One and Only; But
Not for Me; Looking for a Boy; I've Got a Crush on You;
How Long Has This Been Going On?; Maybe; Soon.

Gems from Gershwin

Victor LPT-3055. Jane Froman, Felix Knight, Sunny Skylar,
and orchestra under Shilkret.

Contents: Excerpts from *Of Thee I sing, Girl Crazy, Lady, Be
Good, Tip-Toes, Porgy and Bess,* and others.

Gershwin Jazz Concert

Decca L-5137. Eddie Condon and Orchestra.

Contents: 'S Wonderful; Somebody Loves Me; My One and Only; Oh, Lady, Be Good; Someone to Watch Over Me; The Man I Love; Swanee; I'll Build a Stairway to Paradise.

Gershwin Plays Gershwin

Heritage 0073. George Gershwin at the piano, with Fred Astaire, etc.

Contents: Clap Yo' Hands; Do, Do, Do; Fascinating Rhythm; Sweet and Low Down; Hang On to Me; That Certain Feeling; I'd Rather Charleston; Someone to Watch Over Me; The Half of it, Dearie, Blues.

Gershwin Rarities, Vol. 1

Walden 302. Kaye Ballard, David Craig, Betty Gillett, accompanied by David Baker and John Morris.

Contents: They All Laughed; Things Are Looking Up; Isn't It a Pity? ; Funny Face; Aren't You Kind of Glad We Did? ; Soon; Shall We Dance? ; Stiff Upper Lip; Seventeen and Twenty-one; Kickin' the Clouds.

Gershwin Rarities, Vol. 2

Walden 303. Louise Carlyle, Warren Galjour, accompanied by the John Morris Trio.

Contents: Where's the Boy? ; That Certain Feeling; Let's Kiss and Make Up; Oh, So Nice; I Want to Be a War Bride; Nice Work If You Can Get It; Foggy Day; How Long Has This Been Going On? ; Nightie Night; Sweet and Low Down.

Girl Crazy

Columbia ML-4475. Mary Martin, Louise Carlyle, Eddie Chappell, orchestra and chorus under Engel.

Contents: Overture; Opening Chorus; Bidin' My Time; Could You Use Me?; Broncho Busters; Barbary Coast; Embraceable You; Sam and Delilah; I Got Rhythm; But Not for Me; Treat Me Rough; Boy, What Love Has Done to Me; Cactus Time; Finale.

A Journey to Greatness

Columbia (in preparation). This is a comprehensive Gershwin omnibus including all his serious concert works and over 60 songs from the major musical comedies and motion picture scores.

Music of George Gershwin

Columbia ML-2026. André Kostelanetz and his Orchestra.

Contents: Embraceable You; Fascinating Rhythm; The Man I Love; 'S Wonderful; Maybe; Someone to Watch Over Me; Oh, Lady, Be Good; Soon.

Music of George Gershwin (transcribed for violin)

Decca L-7003. Jascha Heifetz.

Contents: Summertime; A Woman Is a Sometime Thing; My Man's Gone Now; It Ain't Necessarily So; Bess, You Is My Woman Now; Tempo di Blues; Preludes Nos. 1, 2, 3.

Music of George Gershwin

Columbia AAL-39. George Gershwin, Fred Astaire, Hildegarde, Larry Adler, and others.

Contents: The Man I Love; Do, Do, Do; My One and Only; 'S Wonderful; The Half of It, Dearie, Blues; Fascinating Rhythm; Sweet and Low Down; Summertime; Bess, You Is My Woman Now; It Ain't Necessarily So; I Got Plenty o' Nuttin'; There's a Boat That's Leavin' Soon for New York.

Music of George Gershwin (transcribed for four pianos)

Victor LM-125. First Piano Quartet.

Contents: Rhapsody in Blue; Summertime; Bess, You Is My Woman Now; I Got Plenty o' Nuttin'; It Ain't Necessarily So; The Man I Love; Strike Up the Band; An American in Paris.

Of Thee I Sing

Capitol S-350. Jack Carson, Hartman, and the original 1952 Broadway cast. Principal excerpts.

Oscar Peterson and Buddy De Franco Play George Gershwin

Norgran Records. MGM 1016. Orchestra conducted by Russ Garcia, supervised by Norman Granz.

Contents: I Got Rhythm; I Was Doing All Right; The Man I Love; It Ain't Necessarily So; Bess, You Is My Woman Now; Someone to Watch Over Me; 'S Wonderful; Strike Up the Band; They Can't Take That Away from Me.

Songs of George Gershwin

Decca L-508. Bing Crosby.

Contents: Embraceable You; They Can't Take That Away from Me; Love Walked In; Summertime; It Ain't Necessarily So; I Got Plenty o' Nuttin'; Somebody Loves Me; Maybe.

Songs of George Gershwin

Columbia ML-2129. Dorothy Kirsten and Percy Faith and Orchestra.

Contents: Someone to Watch Over Me; Love Walked In; I've Got a Crush on You; Embraceable You; Soon; Do, Do, Do; Love Is Here to Stay; Mine.

Songs of George Gershwin (transcribed for piano)

Columbia CL-6103. Eddy Duchin.

Contents: The Man I Love; Someone to Watch Over Me; Love Walked In; Embraceable You; 'S Wonderful; Somebody Loves Me; Summertime; They Can't Take That Away from Me.

Transcriptions of 18 Songs (transcribed by George Gershwin)

Walden 200. Leonid Hambro.

Contents: Swanee; Nobody But You; I'll Build a Stairway to Paradise; Do It Again; Fascinating Rhythm; Oh, Lady, Be Good; Somebody Loves Me; Sweet and Low Down; That Certain Feeling; The Man I Love; Clap Yo' Hands; Do, Do, Do; My One and Only; 'S Wonderful; Strike Up the Band; Liza; I Got Rhythm.

The Popular Gershwin

Victor LPM-6000. Eddie Fisher, Sauter-Finegan Orchestra, Melachrino Strings, Jaye P. Morgan, June Valli, Dinah Shore, and others.

Contents: Somebody Loves Me; Of Thee I Sing; Love Walked In; Looking for a Boy; Strike Up the Band; Someone to Watch Over Me; Nice Work If You Can Get It; But Not for Me; Love Is Sweeping the Country; I've Got a Crush on You; Do It Again; Let's Call the Whole Thing Off; Embraceable You; I Got Rhythm; Mine; Song of the Flame; Wintergreen for President; They Can't Take That Away from Me; Fascinating Rhythm; Who Cares; I'll Build a Stairway to Paradise; Oh, Lady, Be Good; A Foggy Day; Swanee; How Long Has This Been Going On?; Liza; Bidin' My Time; They All Laughed; 'S Wonderful.

The Serious Gershwin

Victor LM-6033. Morton Gould and his Orchestra, and Morton Gould as piano soloist.

Contents: Rhapsody in Blue; Piano Preludes; Concerto in F; An American in Paris; Porgy and Bess, suite arranged by Gould.

THE WORLD THAT GERSHWIN LIVED IN

GERSHWIN'S LIFE	MUSICAL EVENTS	WORLD EVENTS
		Note—The books and plays named in the year entries below are those that Americans were then talking about: books just published, plays newly produced in this country.
	1885 Jerome Kern b., N. Y. C. 1887 Sigmund Romberg b., Hungary. 1888 Irving Berlin b., Russia. 1890 Paul Whiteman b., Denver. 1892 Ferde Grofé b., N. Y. C. 1896 Ira Gershwin b., N. Y. C. Ragtime introduced at Tony Pastor's.	
1898 Sept. 26, George Gershwin b., Brooklyn.	1898 Sept. 26, *The Fortune-Teller* by Victor Herbert opens in N. Y. C. Sept. 27, Vincent Youmans b., Brooklyn. Also b. this year: Paul Robeson, Roy Harris, Mischa Levitzki. Tin-Pan Alley begins move to 28th St. *A Runaway Girl* by Ivan Caryll opens.	1898 Bismarck d. Hemingway, K. Cornell, B. Lillie, G. Lawrence, b. U. S. war with Spain begins. Curies discover radium. Books: *David Harum* (Westcott), *Elizabeth and Her German Garden* (Arnim), *The Prisoner of Zenda* (Hope), and *Old Chester Tales* (Deland).
	1899 Chausson, J. Strauss the younger, d. Maxie Rosenzweig (Max Rosen) b. In London, world première of *Florodora* by Leslie Stuart (later the composer of *Tipperary*).	1899 U. S. war on the Filipino insurrectos. British war on the Boers in S. Africa. Second Dreyfus trial in France. *In His Steps* (Sheldon), *To Have and To Hold* (Johnston), *Richard Carvel* (Churchill), *Janice Meredith* (Ford).
	1900 Arthur Sullivan d. Weill, Křenek, Copland, Antheil, b. American première of *Florodora*. Sousa, *The Charlatan*. First concert by the Phila. Orchestra.	1900 Paris Exposition. Boxer Rebellion, China. Galveston hurricane. Diesel motor invented. *Fables in Slang* (Ade), *The Reign of Law* (Allen),

1901 Verdi, Ethelbert Nevin, d. Heifetz b. American première of San Toy by Sidney Jones.

1901 At Pan-American Exposition in Buffalo, McKinley fatally shot; T. Roosevelt, President. Queen Victoria d.; Edward VII, King. Dirigible airship invented. Marconi signals letter S across Atlantic by wireless. *Kim* (Kipling), *Crisis* (Churchill), *Mrs. Wiggs of the Cabbage Patch* (Hegan).

1902 Zola d. Radio telephone invented. First radio message sent across the Atlantic. First skyscraper—Flatiron Bldg, N. Y. C. *Just So Stories* (Kipling), *The Virginian* (Wister).

1903 O. Wright makes first successful airplane flight. U. S. recognizes the independent republic of Panama. *The Call of the Wild* (London), *The Pit* (Norris), *The Story of My Life* (Keller).

1904 U. S. acquires and occupies Panama Canal Zone. Perdicaris kidnapped in Tangier. At Louisiana Purchase Exposition (St. Louis) Curtiss makes first public airplane flight. N. Y. subway opened. Russo-Japanese War begins. *The Sea-Wolf* (London), *The Little Shepherd of Kingdom Come* (Fox), *The Garden of Allah* (Hichens).

1902 World premières of Debussy's *Pelléas et Mélisande* and Ravel's *Pavane pour une infante défunte.* Amer. prem. of Debussy's *Afternoon of a Faun. The Prince of Pilsen* by Luders opens.

1903 Caruso's American debut at the Metropolitan Opera House. *Babes in Toyland* (Herbert), *The Geisha* (Jones), *The Wizard of Oz* (Luders).

1904 Dvořák, Emmett (composer of *Dixie*), d. Lily Pons b. Irving Berlin, at 16, begins his career, singing and playing in N. Y. C. restaurants. Premières of Puccini's *Madame Butterfly,* R. Strauss's *Domestic Symphony. The Sho-Gun* (Luders).

1904 At about this time, George starts going to Public School No. 25, at Fifth Avenue and 2d Street, N. Y. C.

GERSHWIN'S LIFE	MUSICAL EVENTS	WORLD EVENTS
	1905 Constant Lambert, Marc Blitzstein, b. Irving Berlin writes his first song, "Marie from Sunny Italy." World première of *The Merry Widow* (Lehár) in Vienna. Herbert's *Mlle. Modiste*.	1905 Lew Wallace, John Hay, Maurice Barrymore, Henry Irving, Joe Jefferson, d. First Russian parliament (Duma) organized. *The Spoilers* (Beach), *The Masquerader* (Thurston).
	1906 Arensky d. Shostakovich b. American première of *Madame Butterfly* (Puccini). *The Red Mill* and *It Happened in Nordland* (Herbert). George Cohan in *George Washington, Jr.*	1906 Ibsen, Carl Schurz, Susan B. Anthony, d. San Francisco earthquake and fire. Thaw tried for murder. Dreyfus found innocent and raised in rank. Alice Roosevelt married in the White House. *The Four Million* (O. Henry), *The House of Mirth* (Wharton), *The Jungle* (Sinclair), *Joseph Vance* (De Morgan), *Lady Baltimore* (Wister).
	1907 Joachim, Grieg, d. Chaliapin's American debut at the Metropolitan. American première of *The Merry Widow* (Lehár). De Forest invents first radio tube and transmits music from N. Y. C. to Navy Yard, Bklyn.	1907 Congress passes the Pure Food and Drugs Act. First Nobel award to an American is given to Michelson (physics). *Three Weeks* (Glyn), *The Shuttle* (Burnett), *Alice-for-Short* (De Morgan), *The Ancestors* (Atherton).
1908 In this year or the next, George meets Maxie Rosenzweig, and they begin their friendship.	1908 Sarasate, Rimsky-Korsakov, MacDowell, d. World première of *The Chocolate Soldier* (Straus). *The Rose of Algeria* (Herbert).	1908 Financial panic in the U. S. Hudson River Tunnel opens. *Old Wives' Tale* (Bennett), *The Blue Bird* (Maeterlinck).

1909 Taft inaugurated. Peary reaches the North Pole. First dirigible balloon race. Blériot flies across the English Channel. Maxim silencer invented. *The Trail of the Lonesome Pine* (Fox), *A Girl of the Limberlost* (Porter).

1910 Deaths: Julia Ward Howe, Florence Nightingale, Mark Twain, O. Henry, and Henri Dunant (founder, 1864, of International Red Cross). King Edward VII d., George V becomes King. *The Rosary* (Barclay).

1911 Glenn Curtiss builds the first hydroplane. First U. S. transcontinental flight: N. Y.-Pasadena, 84 hours. Roosevelt Dam completed. *The Harvester* (Porter), *Queed* (Harrison).

1912 Deaths: Clara Barton, Dr. Joseph Lister, Gen. Wm. Booth, Capt. Robert F. Scott. First Balkan War. China becomes a republic under Sun Yat-sen. *Titanic* sunk by iceberg.

1913 Floods in Ohio and Indiana. Woodrow Wilson begins his first term. Peace Palace at The Hague dedicated. Second Balkan War. *Pollyanna* (Porter).

1909 Albéniz d. American première of *The Chocolate Soldier* (Straus). *Giovinezza* written, later to be adopted as the official Fascist hymn.

1910 Balakirev d. First experimental opera broadcast from the Metropolitan: part of *Pagliacci* with Caruso. *Naughty Marietta* (Herbert). *Madame Sherry* (Hoschna).

1911 Mahler d. In St. Petersburg the debut of Heifetz, aged 10. Berlin publishes his first successes, "Alexander's Ragtime Band" and "Everybody's Doin' It." *The Pink Lady* (Caryll).

1912 Massenet, Coleridge-Taylor, d. American prem. of *The Firefly* (Friml). First "blues" song published—W. C. Handy's "Memphis Street Blues."

1913 Berlin writes "International Rag." S. Romberg comes to the U. S. to live. American première of *Der Rosenkavalier* (R. Strauss). *Sweethearts* (Herbert).

1910 The Gershwin family buys a piano, and George begins to take lessons.

1913 George gets his first job—as a song-plugger at Remick's.

GERSHWIN'S LIFE	MUSICAL EVENTS	WORLD EVENTS
	1914 W. C. Handy's "St. Louis Blues" published. World première of Stravinsky's *Rite of Spring*. Sibelius visits the U. S. Irving Berlin's first complete show, *Watch Your Step*.	1914 Panama Canal opened to traffic. Assassination of Archduke Rudolf leads to outbreak of World War I. *Penrod* (Tarkington), *Pygmalion* (Shaw), *Tarzan of the Apes* (Burroughs), *The Inside of the Cup* (Churchill).
	1915 Goldmark d. Première of Carpenter's *Adventures in a Perambulator*. *Princess Pat* (Herbert). *Katinka* (Friml). Jerome Kern's first success, *Very Good, Eddie*.	1915 Booker Washington, Charles Frohman, Dr. Paul Ehrlich, d. Orson Welles b. Panama-Pacific Expos. in San Francisco. *Lusitania* sunk by German submarine. *Ruggles of Red Gap* (Wilson), *The Sea Hawk* (Sabatini), *Of Human Bondage* (Maugham).
1916 Gershwin's first song is published by Harry Von Tilzer: "When You Want 'Em You Can't Get 'Em." First song on Broadway, "Making of a Girl," is in Romberg's *Passing Show of 1916*.	1916 Granados d. Menuhin b. First use of the word "jazz" in print, when *Variety* reports jazz bands in Chicago. American premières of Stravinsky's *Petrouchka* and *The Fire Bird*.	1916 Jack London d. Depth bomb invented. Tank invented. U. S. troops enter Mexico and pursue Villa. *Spoon River Anthology* (Masters), *Seventeen* (Tarkington), *El Supremo* (White).
1917 Serves as rehearsal pianist for *Miss 1917* (Herbert and Kern). Gives up his Remick job. Tries several others. Accompanist for Louise Dresser on tour. Is offered, and refuses, job as secretary to Irving Berlin.	1917 First jazz records are made (Victor). First jazz band in N. Y. C. *Oh, Boy* and *Have a Heart* (Kern). *Yip, Yip, Yaphank* (Berlin). *Cohan Revue* (Cohan and Kern). *Maytime* (Romberg).	1917 Zeppelin, Buffalo Bill, d. Wilson begins his second term. Russian revolution and republic. U. S. enters World War. Prohibition Amendment passed. *Mr. Britling Sees It Through* (Wells), *Renascence* (Millay).

1918 Rostand, John L. Sullivan, d. Czar and family assassinated. Soviets adopt a constitution. Flu epidemic. World War I ends. Woman Suffrage Amendment passed. *Four Horsemen of the Apocalypse* (Blasco Ibáñez).

1919 Carnegie, d. Peace treaty signed at Versailles. First plane crossings of the Atlantic eastward: Alcock and Brown fly non-stop to Ireland, and Navy seaplane NC4 to Portugal. Weimar Constitution promulgated in Germany. *The Moon and Sixpence* (Maugham), *Jurgen* (Cabell).

1920 Peary d. Volstead Act goes into force. Women vote. First Assembly of the League of Nations, Geneva. *Main Street* (Lewis), *Outline of History* (Wells), *Relativity* (Einstein), *Miss Lulu Bett* (Gale), *Psychoanalysis* (Freud), *Economic Consequences of the Peace* (Keynes).

1921 Harding inaugurated. Panama Canal officially completed. *If Winter Comes* (Hutchinson), *Alice Adams* (Tarkington), *Story of Mankind* (Van Loon), *Queen Victoria* (Strachey).

1918 Debussy, César Cui, d. First jazz-band concerts in Paris. Columbia starts making jazz records. Berlin writes the first of his *Ziegfeld Follies*.

1919 Leoncavallo, Adelina Patti, d. Paderewski becomes premier of Poland. Première of *Through the Looking-Glass* by Deems Taylor. *Ziegfeld Follies* (Berlin).

1920 Caruso's final performance at the Metropolitan (see 1921). First U. S. commercial radio station opens, WWJ, Detroit. *Sally* (Kern). *Ziegfeld Follies* (Berlin).

1921 Caruso, Humperdinck, Saint-Saëns, d. World première of Prokofiev's *Love for Three Oranges*. *Blossom Time* (Romberg). Berlin's *Music Box Revue* (first of a series through 1925).

1918 Gets job as composer for Max Dreyfus, music publisher. Songs taken for *Look Who's Here* and *Hitchy-Koo*. "The Real American Folk Song" used in *Ladies First*. First all-Gershwin show, *Half-Past Eight*, not successful.

1919 His first success, *La La Lucille*, opens on Broadway. Songs used in *Dere Mable* and *Broadway Brevities*.

1920 "Swanee" transformed into a hit by Al Jolson. George begins five years of writing the *Scandals* music (1920-24). Contributes songs to *Good Morning, Judge*; *The Sweetheart Shop*; *Ed Wynn's Carnival*; *The Lady in Red*; *Blue Eyes*.

1921 Writes the *Scandals of 1921*. Has songs in *The Midnight Whirl* and *A Dangerous Maid*. At about this time the Gershwin family move uptown to 110th St. and Amsterdam Ave.

GERSHWIN'S LIFE	MUSICAL EVENTS	WORLD EVENTS
1922 One of Gershwin's songs in his *Scandals of 1922* is "I'll Build a Stairway to Paradise." For *The French Doll* he writes "Do It Again." Writes *Our Nell.* Has songs in *For Goodness' Sake* and *The Nifties.* Beryl Rubinstein calls him "a great composer."	1922 B.B.C. begins broadcasting concerts. Zez Confrey's *Kitten on the Keys* is one of the last "ragtime" works. Hollywood Bowl concerts begin. American première of Stravinsky's *Rite of Spring. The Student Prince* (Romberg).	1922 Alexander Graham Bell d. First air crossing from Europe to Brazil. Fourteen Russian republics combine as the U.S.S.R. *Gentle Julia* (Tarkington), *Babbitt* (Lewis), *The Covered Wagon* (Hough), *The Forsyte Saga* (Galsworthy).
1923 Eva Gauthier sings four Gershwin songs at her recital. George writes music for the *Rainbow Revue* and *Sweet Little Devil.* In his music for the *Scandals* is the short play *135th Street.* Whiteman asks him to compose a large symphonic-jazz work.	1923 Première of Schelling's *A Victory Ball.* Paul Whiteman and his band are featured in *The Scandals of 1923.*	1923 Sarah Bernhardt d. Harding d.; Coolidge becomes President. Earthquake in Japan. French and Belgian troops occupy the Ruhr. Revolt in Bavaria, organized by Hindenburg and Hitler —Munich "Putsch"—Hitler captured and jailed. Autogiro invented. *Black Oxen* (Atherton).
1924 His *Scandals of 1924* includes "Somebody Loves Me." Première of the *Rhapsody in Blue* at Aeolian Hall with Whiteman. Writes *Lady, Be Good* ("The Man I Love" being in the early performances only). Goes to London to produce *Primrose* and *Stop Flirting.*	1924 Victor Herbert, Puccini, d. First Carnegie Hall concert of Whiteman's band; he tours continent playing symphonic jazz. Orthophonic phonograph invented. Première of Honegger's *Pacific 231. Rose Marie* (Friml).	1924 Wilson, Lenin, d. Prince of Wales makes American tour, his party including Lord and Lady Louis Mountbatten. Dawes Reparation Plan accepted. Dirigible ZR3 flies from Germany to the U. S. Play: *What Price Glory?* Books: *So Big* (Ferber), *Saint Joan* (Shaw), *When We Were Very Young* (Milne).

1925 Première of the Concerto in F, with Gershwin as piano soloist, Damrosch conducting, at Carnegie Hall. Writes *Tell Me More*, *Tip-Toes*, and *Song of the Flame*

1926 Writes *Oh Kay*. Composes the *Preludes* for piano.

1927 First all-Gershwin program is given by the Philharmonic-Symphony Orchestra at the Stadium under Hoogstraten, Gershwin being soloist in the *Rhapsody in Blue* and the Concerto in F. Premières of *Rosalie*, *Strike Up the Band*, and *Funny Face*.

1925 Premières of Copland's *Music for the Theatre*, Alban Berg's *Wozzeck*, Antheil's *Ballet Mécanique*. *Sunny* (Kern), *No, No, Nanette* (Youmans), *The Vagabond King* (Friml).

1926 Whiteman tours Europe with his band; his autobiography *Jazz* published. N.B.C. broadcasts its first music program. *Sea Beast* opens in N. Y. C., earliest musical film, music recorded separately and then synchronized with the silent film (see 1927). Première of Walton's *Façade* and Carpenter's *Skyscrapers*.

1927 Opening of *The Jazz Singer*, first musical film to have music and photography simultaneously recorded. Columbia Broadcasting System opens. Dynamic loudspeaker invented. Premières of Weill's *Mahagonny* and Krenek's *Jonny spielt auf*. *Hit the Deck* (Youmans), *Desert Song* (Romberg), *Show Boat* (Kern).

1925 Bryan d. Coolidge begins second term. Scopes trial in Tennessee. Navy dirigible *Shenandoah* wrecked. Submarine S51 sunk off R. I. coast. Locarno Treaties signed. *An American Tragedy* (Dreiser), *The Constant Nymph* (Kennedy), *The Matriarch* (Stern), *Arrowsmith* (Lewis), *Beau Geste* (Wren).

1926 Burbank, President Eliot, Valentino, Houdini, d. Byrd flies to North Pole. General strike in Britain. Germany admitted to the League of Nations. Delaware Bridge completed, Camden-Phila. *Show Boat* (Ferber), *The Sun Also Rises* (Hemingway), *Sorrell and Son* (Deeping).

1927 John Drew d. Sacco and Vanzetti executed. Civil war in China. Lindbergh's solo flight across the Atlantic. Mississippi floods. Submarine S4 sunk off Provincetown, Mass. Theatre Guild produces Heyward's play *Porgy*. *Death Comes for the Archbishop* (Cather), *Elmer Gantry* (Lewis).

GERSHWIN'S LIFE	MUSICAL EVENTS	WORLD EVENTS
1928 Writes *Treasure Girl*. Goes to Europe, finds the *Rhapsody* being given as a ballet and played at a symphony concert in Paris. Writes *An American in Paris*, and it has its première in N. Y. C. in December.	1928 In Paris, the world première of Ravel's *Bolero*. *The New Moon* (Romberg). *The Three Musketeers* (Friml).	1928 Russia begins work on Five-Year Plan. *Graf Zeppelin* crosses from Germany to the U. S. Color-photography process invented. *The Bridge of San Luis Rey* (Wilder), *The Case of Sergeant Grischa* (Zweig).
1929 Writes *Show Girl*. Conducts *An American in Paris* at a Lewisohn Stadium summer concert. Conducts a concert of the Manhattan Symphony Orchestra. In Boston conducts *Strike Up the Band!*	1929 Première of Constant Lambert's *Rio Grande*. American première of Křenek's *Jonny spielt auf*. *Sweet Adeline* (Kern). *Great Day* (Youmans).	1929 Hoover inaugurated. Vatican City established. Byrd's Antarctic expedition. Kellogg-Briand Treaty signed by Powers. Stock-market crash in late October starts world depression. *Dodsworth* (Lewis), *All Quiet on the Western Front* (Remarque).
1930 Writes *Girl Crazy*. At a Stadium concert in August, is soloist in his Concerto in F and conducts *Rhapsody in Blue*, and conducts *An American in Paris*.	1930 Premières of Antheil's opera *Transatlantic* and ballet *Flight*, and of Stravinsky's *Symphony of Psalms*. Toscanini and the N. Y. Philharmonic tour Europe.	1930 Rhineland evacuated by the French. Young Plan for reparations announced. Sheriff's play *Journey's End*. *Cimarron* (Ferber).
1931 Writes *Of Thee I Sing*. In the winter of 1930-31 goes to Hollywood to write his first musical film, *Delicious*, produced this year. Writes his *Second Rhapsody*. In London, *An American in Paris* is played at an ISCM festival.	1931 Melba, Ysaye, Vincent d'Indy, d. First nationwide broadcast of an entire opera—*Hänsel and Gretel*, from the Metropolitan. Amer. prem. of Weinberger's *Schwanda*. *The Cat and the Fiddle* (Kern). *Bitter Sweet* (Coward). *The Band Wagon* (Schwartz).	1931 Joffre, Pavlova, Belasco, Edison, d. Lindberghs fly to Japan and China. World Powers begin to go off gold standard. King of Siam visits N. Y. C. Empire State Bldg. completed. *The Good Earth* (Buck), *Cakes and Ale* (Maugham).

1932 Writes *Pardon My English*. His *Second Rhapsody* has première with the Boston Symphony, Gershwin as soloist. Writes the *Cuban Overture* and conducts its première. Pulitzer Prize awarded to *Of Thee I Sing*.

1933 Writes *Let 'Em Eat Cake*.

1934 Goes on tour of the country conducting concerts of popular music.

1935 His folk opera *Porgy and Bess* opens in Boston on Sept. 30, and in New York on Oct. 10.

1932 Gadski, Sousa, d. Radio City Music Hall opens. *Face the Music* (Berlin). *Cavalcade* (Coward).

1933 Elgar, Holst, Delius, d. Première of Louis Gruenberg's opera *Emperor Jones*. *Music in the Air* (Kern). *Roberta* (Kern). *As Thousands Cheer* (Berlin).

1934 Mutual Broadcasting System opens. Première of Roy Harris's *When Johnny Comes Marching Home*.

1935 Sembrich, Ippolitov-Ivanov, Alban Berg, d. Nazis bar Jews from German orchestras. In U. S., swing music becomes popular. Federal Music Project established.

1932 Amelia Earhart flies to Ireland. Mayor Walker of N. Y. C. resigns while being tried by Gov. Roosevelt. St. Lawrence power project inaugurated. Lindbergh baby murdered. *Mutiny on the Bounty* (Nordhoff and Hall).

1933 F. D. Roosevelt begins first term. Century of Progress Exposition, Chicago. "Technocracy." Disney's *Three Little Pigs*. Prohibition repealed. Reichstag fire in Berlin. *Anthony Adverse* (Allen), *Life Begins at Forty* (Pitkin).

1934 Dionne quintuplets b. *Morro Castle* burned. Television invented. Hitler becomes Führer. Dollfuss assassinated by Nazis in Vienna. Italy invades Ethiopia. *Ulysses* (Joyce), *Good-bye, Mr. Chips* (Hilton).

1935 Deaths: Will Rogers, Jane Addams, Dreyfus, Justice O. W. Holmes. Lindbergh murderer executed. Japan withdraws from the League. German Jews lose citizenship. Quezon becomes president of the Philippines. U. S. Social Security Act passed. *It Can't Happen Here* (Lewis).

GERSHWIN'S LIFE	MUSICAL EVENTS	WORLD EVENTS
1936 Returns to Hollywood to write music for films. His film *Shall We Dance?* is produced this year.	1936 Deaths: Scotti, Respighi, Glazunov, Gabrilowitsch, Schumann-Heink, Rubin Goldmark. Première of Prokofiev's *Peter and the Wolf.* Barbirolli engaged as conductor of the N. Y. Philharmonic-Symphony Orchestra.	1936 George V d. (Jan.). Edward VIII succeeds; abdicates (Dec.). George VI succeeds. Italians victorious in Ethiopia. Revolt against Spanish Republic starts in Morocco, spreads to Spain. General Chiang kidnaped in China. Germans reoccupy Rhineland. Inter-American Conference, Buenos Aires. Moscow trials and executions. *Gone with the Wind* (Mitchell), *How to Win Friends and Influence People* (Carnegie).
1937 The David Bispham Medal is awarded to *Porgy and Bess*. Musical films written and produced this year are *A Damsel in Distress* and *The Goldwyn Follies*. In July, a collapse is followed by serious illness and an operation. Gershwin dies in Hollywood on July 11. Funeral and burial in New York on July 15.	193* Ravel d. N.B.C. Symphony Orchestra broadcasts its first concert. First telecast of an entire opera by B.B.C. Premières of Copland's *Music for Radio*, Alban Berg's opera *Lulu*, and Marc Blitzstein's opera *The Cradle Will Rock.*	1937 King George and Queen Elizabeth crowned. Duke of Windsor marries Mrs. Warfield. F. D. Roosevelt begins second term. Mississippi Valley floods. Amelia Earhart lost. Soviet plane lands at North Pole. Hitler repudiates Versailles Treaty. Japan begins war on China. *Hindenburg* destroyed on landing at Lakehurst, N. J.

Index